The Illusion of Economic Stability

The Illusion of
Economic Stability

Eli Ginzberg

With a new introduction by
Robert M. Solow

Transaction Publishers
New Brunswick (U.S.A.) and London (U.K.)

Library of Congress Catalog Number: 2003044786
ISBN: 0-7658-0548-0
Printed in the United States of America

Library of Congress Cataloging-in-Publication Data

Ginzberg, Eli, 1911-
    The illusion of economic stability / Eli Ginzberg ; with a new introduction
    by Robert M. Solow.
        Originally published: New York : Harper & Brothers, 1939.
        Includes bibliographical references and index.
        ISBN 0-7658-0548-0 (pbk.)
            1. United States—Economic conditions—1918-1945. 2. Business
    cycles. I. Title.

HC106.3.G5 2003
330.973'091—dc21   2003044786

To

My Mother

Contents

TRANSACTION INTRODUCTION ix

PREFACE xxi

INTRODUCTION 1

Part I. BIRTH OF THE ILLUSION
I. THE TRADITION OF BUSINESS OPTIMISM 11

Part II. GROWTH OF THE ILLUSION
II. THE STABILIZATION OF THE INDIVIDUAL CONCERN 31

Part III. MATURITY OF THE ILLUSION
III. THE DOCTRINE OF HIGH WAGES 51
IV. SIGNPOSTS OF STABILITY 69
V. THE BANKING MECHANISM 96
VI. THE NEW ERA 114

Part IV. SENESCENCE OF THE ILLUSION
VII. THE DEPRESSION 143
VIII. THE NEW DEAL 171

Part V. DEATH OF THE ILLUSION
IX. STABILITY AND CHANGE 211

APPENDIXES 247
NOTES 259
INDEX OF NAMES 275

vii

Transaction Introduction

One risk that comes with a very long and very productive career is the likelihood that even fairly attentive readers may eventually forget that writer's earlier work, or not even know that it exists. It is a safe guess that many think of Eli Ginzberg mainly as a contributor to the literature on the distribution of healthcare, or as a participant in the public discussion on the labor-force participation of women and minorities and other aspects of manpower policy. Some will know that the precocious Ginzberg's first book—published when he was twenty-two—was a study of Adam Smith and his immediate predecessors and successors in political economy.

At just about that time he was awarded a traveling fellowship, and used it to go about the country interviewing high officers of a number of major corporations—mostly, but not entirely, manufacturing companies, as would have been natural for the period. One of the products of that enterprise is the present book, *The Illusion of Economic Stability*, first published in 1939, when the (still-precocious) author was twenty-eight, and the depression of the 1930s was barely at an end. As a tribute to my old friend, I now discuss this book. It is not at all like archetypical Ginzberg either in content or in style, but I think it does have some intellectual or attitudinal affinities to the later and more familiar work of its author.

It was not this sort of continuity, however, that led me to *The Illusion of Economic Stability*, but rather a different kind of historical artifact. We now tend to think of the long boom of the 1920s as the prologue to, or even the origin of, the crash of 1929 and the depression of the 1930s. Of course, the business-executive protagonists and, with very few outliers, the standard contemporary commentators on the scene did not see it that way. The phrase that was coined at the time to encapsulate the long prosperity was "The New Era." Now *that* rings a bell. It would have taken only a stray neuron fired a millisecond earlier to have invented instead an alternative slogan—like "The New Economy" just for instance. That is the parallel between the 1920s and the 1990s that interests me.

Needless to say—as one normally says of something that needs to be said—the mostly manufacturing-based, and still non-trivially agricultural, economy of the 1920s has little texture in common with the much richer, technologically more advanced, and mostly service-based economy of the 1990s. The particular common response that I want to discuss is the belief that somehow the rules and generalizations had changed, that the future would be utterly unlike the past, that the new era (economy) was *sui generis*.

Here I want to be clear about my own take on the meta-question. The young Ginzberg is plainly cynical about all that careless talk of The New Era. He can suppress the occasional sarcasm only with difficulty, and sometimes not at all. (Remember that he was writing in 1939 after two downturns and ten years of depression.) It is not so clear whether his preferred view is that (a) the basic truths of economic theory are, if not eternal, at least enduring, and unlikely to make a convenient exception for the new era, or that (b) any talk of enduring abstract truth is its own illusion, and mildly analytical description is as deep as it gets. On that second view, the New Era talk was a fatuous error, but might conceivably have turned out to be valid. On the first, it was intrinsically implausible from the word "go."

Unlike the young—or the old—Ginzberg, I am a model-builder by inclination and training. I like to quote the Oxford philosopher John Austin who said something like: "One would be tempted to call oversimplification the occupational disease of philosophers if it were not their occupation." So too for economic theorists. But I believe rather strongly that the "right" model for an occasion depends on the context—the institutional context, of course—but also on the current mix of beliefs, attitudes, norms, and "theories" that inhabits the minds of businessmen, bankers, consumers, and savers. In this way, I end up not so far from the young Ginzberg, though not exactly in the same place.

A subsidiary analogy between the 1920s and the 1990s is the significance of the stock market boom that characterized each period. *The Illusion of Economic Stability* does not dwell in a serious way on finance-theoretic insights into the bull market of the 1920s, and I do not want to make any refined analogy with the 1990s. But I do want to comment in due course on the young Ginzberg's observation that he had witnessed an episode of what he could fairly have called "irrational exuberance," if that phrase had occurred to him.

Speaking of phrases, I want to comment very briefly on the style and tone of the book. The prose is tighter and more aphoristic than later Ginzberg, and the tone is more detached, even sardonic. I do not know where this came from, if it came from anywhere in particular. Young Ginzberg certainly did not imbibe it from mentors like A. F. Burns and J. M. Clark, although some of his ideas about business cycles do come from them, as will be seen. I hear a little Thorstein Veblen in the prose, and indeed Veblen is cited more than once. The style is not the man, really, so no inference is to be drawn. But the observation is worth making.

If an illusion of economic stability suffused the 1920s, summed up in the phrase about The New Era, what was its origin? The first 28 or 29 percent of the twentieth century were, on the whole, pretty good years, especially contrasted with the two major depressions of the 1870s and 1890s. It is true that there had been a very sharp and painful recession just after the First World War; but, as Ginzberg points out, that could be categorized as war-related and therefore extrinsic, and not part of the inescapable normal shape of things.

True enough, as Ginzberg says, but he then goes on to offer a less obvious and more interesting suggestion. During the early 1920s the "scientific management" movement hatched the notion that seasonal unemployment and the parallel excess capacity could be smoothed away by regular production for stock. Notice that this was a firm-by-firm proposition, not a macroeconomic stabilization scheme, although stability at the firm level would imply aggregate stability. To be able to use inventories to buffer production from seasonal shifts in demand, firms would have to offer price incentives or other rewards to buyers who would commit to long-term purchase agreements. Alternatively, they could integrate forward, absorb retail outlets, and again pursue price variation to smooth production.

Apparently these efforts met with some success. Young Ginzberg notes that *that* may have been an illusion, induced by the generally buoyant macroeconomic trend. Even so, one can see how business executives might have told their interlocutor that they had in fact found the key to stability of sales, profit, and employment.

Another possible contributor to this mind-set was the "doctrine of high wages." That pat phrase set off a vague echo in my head, but it is a doctrine that has not survived. It was live at the time, according to young Dr. Ginzberg. He reports that sticky nominal wages and falling prices after the slump of 1920-21 left real wages fairly high. This state of affairs proved compatible with prosperity, despite earlier calls from the business community for rolling back wartime wage gains.

The natural explanation was that American manufacturing had achieved high productivity gains and unprecedented efficiency. Foreigners came to observe and admire. A virtuous-circle argument then went on to claim that high wages were actually necessary for a high productivity economy, because they created the mass market that was needed to buy the resulting flood of goods and allow the exploitation of scale economies. It appears that more than a few employers bought into this idea.

In actuality, nominal and real wages rose only very slowly after 1924. The doctrine of high wages rested neither on theory nor on practice, but on faith. The young and already cynical Ginzberg commented that "...more important than the facts were the encomia showered upon the doctrine by labor and capital alike. Criticism can seldom withstand enthusiasm, for enthusiasm is always strongly motivated." That does not sound like the diplomatic sage we celebrate today. The young Dr. Ginzberg apparently had a sharp tongue in his mouth. Besides, it has to be admitted that there was an ample supply of tempting targets. The same could be said about similar effusions today. Maybe there is something about periods of prosperity that encourages "enthusiasm." If you like to look for parallels between The New Era and The New Economy, this might be one.

If the young Ginzberg already knew that perpetual economic stability is and was an illusion, he must have had an inkling why. It is clear from the text what sort of theory of the business cycle was in his head. The main influences were his teachers, Arthur F. Burns (especially *Production Trends in the United States since 1870* [1934]) and John Maurice Clark (especially *Strategic Factors in Business Cycles* [1934]). He had also absorbed Wesley C. Mitchell's *Business Cycles* (1927) and Frederic C. Mills's *Economic Tendencies* (1932), but they seemed to play a somewhat smaller role in his thinking.

There is a faint aroma of Morningside Heights about this collection of influences. I do not know enough to judge whether it reflects a little Columbia University parochialism or merely the absence of any other contemporary guides to the understanding of economic fluctuations. There are a few references to J. M. Keynes's *General Theory of Employment, Interest and Money* (1936) in the second half of the book. But it is not surprising that the Keynesian way of looking at prosperity and depression had not penetrated systematically into Ginzberg's thinking. I know from experience that a freshman taking an elementary course in economics 200 miles north of Manhattan in 1940-41 would have been entirely innocent of any notion about aggregate demand.

Instead *Illusion* emphasizes the idea that any major goods-producing industry in a national economy will trace out a lifecycle beginning with accelerating growth and ending in retardation, saturation, and sometimes even decline. In the case of The New Era in the United States, the principal actors in this drama were the automobile and construction industries, with smaller roles played by electric utilities and the producers of household durables. The main initiating factor was the S-shaped industrial life cycle learned from Burns; and the main transmission mechanism was the acceleration principle learned from Clark. These forces, Ginzberg suggests, were far too strong to be countered by the froth that made up the talk of a New Era.

From this view, the prosperity of the 1920s was carried mainly by the diffusion of the automobile and its accessories, the building of a street and highway network, and the consumption expenditures of the enlarged traveling public as well as the investment expenditures of the businesses that catered to the needs of the traveling public. The consequent shrinking of distance, combined with the growth of the population (natural increase plus immigration), in turn encouraged a boom in both public and private construction, along with a complementary demand for the articles that furnish a house, a store, an office, or a factory.

Any such boom will eventually run up against the limits of space, of need, of a lack of new buyers. There is no reason why autos and construction should be replaced by some other industries at just the right time. As soon as the leading industries start to slow down, however, the industries that provide them with plants and equipment will experience absolute declines, because the demand for investment goods is proportioned to the increase in the output of the leading industries. An industry whose production grows *more slowly* needs *less* new capacity. And so the downturn comes.

This kind of account would not carry so much analytical conviction today. It might do as an after-the-fact description once a downturn has occurred. Not all industries will turn down together; those that do will slow before they contract; and the acceleration principle will magnify the effect on the capital-goods sectors. But the analogy to inevitable, almost biological, senescence is not so convincing. We are now more likely to think that income and expenditure can expand together, while the built in, though irregular force of innovation leads to new industries and therefore new objects of expenditure. The dynamics of this process can be very complicated. The business cycle seems less like a determinate sequence, and even less so when it is amplified or damped by the credit mechanism (as the young Ginzberg knew perfectly well).

To take the obvious contemporary analogy: what looks (at the beginning of the twenty-first century) like the end of the New-Economy boom in the U.S. will very likely take the form of a retardation and then a contraction in the production of computers and peripherals. At least it is the bad news in the sales and profits of Compaq, Dell, and IBM, as well as the glamorous software producers that captured the headlines. But a modern macroeconomist would not be content with an explanation that rested on a simple "sooner or later it was bound to happen" argument. Some sort of complete, self-contained model would be required, equilibrium-style or disequilibrium-style. The modern fashion in macroeconomics would not take the aging of a basic industry as an exogenous event requiring no further explanation.

It is worth noting that Eli Ginzberg could not be expected to think in those terms in 1939; the intellectual infrastructure was just in the wings. It is also worth noting that a good causal account of the depression of the 1930s is still a matter of professional controversy, model or no model. What Ginzberg found worse than implausible was the addled belief that it could never happen.

Addled beliefs we have always with us, and they may even have a family resemblance over a time span as long as that between the 1920s and the 1990s. That similarity might be explained by a common source in wishful thinking. Deeper analogies between The New Era and The New Economy are rather less convincing. On the evidence of his book, the young Ginzberg was not given to facile historical parallels.

The very high rate of business investment in the 1990s reflected large purchases of information processing equipment and software, even more so if some communications equipment is added. That category accounted for less than a quarter of non-residential fixed investment in 1991, but just about half in the last quarter of 2000. Headlines suggested that the computer and software industries would be major carriers of the slowdown and downturn of the early 2000s. The prominently displayed bad news came from IBM and Dell and Compaq, and Cisco and Yahoo, not to mention the easy-come-easy-go dot.coms.

Is the computer-software complex the source of the economic softness, or does it just reflect sharp deceleration elsewhere? It will take a longer run of data before any careful analysis can be done, but that is not the point I want to make here. It seems very unlikely that medium-to-long-run saturation can be the core of the story of the end of the 1990s, as Ginzberg thought it was at the end of the 1920s. The uses of computers and software seem to be much more open-ended than the uses of automobiles and construction. The analogy to a population of fruit flies expanding into a limited space seems much less appropriate now than it may have been then. On the other hand, the acceleration principle still rings true. It is hardly cause for surprise if the slowdown of consumer spending—which was being actively sought by the Federal Reserve and wished for by others— should be reflected in an absolute decline in the most popular form of investment.

Ginzberg was careful not to dwell on the stock market, and I shall follow his sound example: too volatile, too psychological, too tenuously connected to fundamentals, in the short run at least. It is probably safe to say, however, that the "real" economy and the level of the stock market are not independent of one another. The connection—between the cost of capital and investment, and between personal wealth and consumption—may be somewhat closer today than it was in The New Era, mainly because nowadays a vastly larger fraction of all families owns some equities, directly or through pension funds. If a volatile stock market has an influence on aggregate spending, that is one more reason why the illusion of (automatic) economic stability has much the same status today as it did when Eli Ginzberg wrote. It would be a mistake collectively to forget what we had learned in the meanwhile about the need to work at macroeconomic stabilization.

ROBERT M. SOLOW

Preface

During the nineteen twenties, a group of enterprising corporations attempted to stabilize their production and employment. Since little was known of these experiments and still less of the impress of the depression upon them, an investigation suggested itself. After spending the summer of 1933 in a study of Eastman Kodak, Hickey-Freeman, Endicott-Johnson, General Electric, Dennison Manufacturing Company, each of whom had some right to be classed among the pioneers, it became clear to me that these experiments, though highly interesting, were of limited significance. I therefore spent the remainder of the year accumulating data on the postwar developments of the American economy, especially as these data were reflected in the experiences of representative concerns in the following industries: steel, automobile, rubber tire, farm implement, soap, canning, cotton goods, motion picture, lumber, mining, petroleum, dairy products. Only the generous assistance of executives and employees made these studies possible and, although detailed acknowledgments would be difficult, my indebtedness is great.

The welter of materials and impressions did not easily permit of systematization; the relations between the data were far from obvious. The original study had been planned as *The Stabilization of American Industry* but my notes were heavily weighted with facts and figures

PREFACE

about economic instability, for the most serious depression in the country's history had just begun to lift. A reworking of the materials led to the emergence of a new theme: *The Illusion of Economic Stability.*

The award of the William Bayard Cutting Traveling Fellowship for 1933-34 made possible the field investigation. The Columbia University Council for Research in the Social Sciences, under the chairmanship of the late Howard Lee McBain, appropriated funds to facilitate the writing of this book, for which subvention I am deeply grateful.

Since the actions of the market are legion, they can never be comprehended in their entirety. At best, the raw data of economics can be selected and arranged with an aim to discover significant relations among strategic factors. To give form to the inchoate is always dangerous, for the investigator's unconscious influences every pattern. Yet the subjective can be restrained. In the following pages deliberate effort has been made to weave the patterns around the facts. Although inferences have not been avoided and inferences, by definition, go beyond the facts, it is hoped that no inference goes contrary to the facts.

In the search for synthesis reliance upon experts is mandatory. Only the detailed research of previous students, and the ability to borrow liberally from their findings, made possible the completion of this book. The notes indicate the extent of my indebtedness. In particular, I received assistance from Dr. Moses Abramovitz of Harvard University and Dr. Harry George Friedman of General American Investors.

PREFACE

From start to finish it was my good fortune to have the active cooperation of Professor Leo Wolman, who outlined the field investigation, secured the grant from the Columbia University Council for Research in the Social Sciences, and enriched the manuscript by valuable suggestions.

To my former teachers Professors John Maurice Clark, Frederick Mills and Wesley Mitchell I am especially grateful for their careful reading of the manuscript and for their many corrections and additions. Professor Benjamin Beckhart, Mr. Rollin Bennett, Dr. Raymond Saulnier and Professor Carl Shoup have also offered me valuable counsel. The readability of the manuscript was increased by Professor Frederick Fassett, Jr., of the Massachusetts Institute of Technology who was kind enough to submit my prose to his expert scrutiny.

ELI GINZBERG

NEW YORK, OCTOBER, 1938.

INTRODUCTION

Eat, drink, and be merry is the counsel of Ecclesiastes; but man, fool that he is, insists upon fretting about the future of his soul. Held prisoner by fears, he can seldom act rationally. He warns his children of the dangers of indulgence and then spends his days stinting himself so that he may transfer to them hoards of earthly possessions. In a world such as this, it is scarcely surprising that the course of events is as much influenced by visions of the future as it is limited by conditions of the past.

Business enterprise is no exception. The market moves in response to myriad purchases and sales, the vast majority of which are entered into by traders under pressures so relentless that they cannot be ignored. Yet every exchange is not dictated. Many are executed with an eye more to future advantage than to present necessity. But the future is unknown and, at best, the present can be studied only in the hope that it may suggest a clue or two. Serious difficulties confront the student of the present, for he can differentiate between the growing and the dying, between the strong and impotent, only by the use of attitudes. Admixtures of experience and reflection, attitudes are always prisoners of the past. More likely than not, they will prove insensitive to the new, especially when the new is embryonic. So long as economic development depends not only upon automatic responses to momentary

1

stimuli but also upon present evaluations of future prospects, error will remain integral to economic reality. Not until men become prophets will this partnership between the true and the false, between the illusory and the real, be broken. The record shows that it is an association of long standing.

In the late fall of 1928, an executive of a mammoth merchandising concern sold every share of stock that he owned, for he felt assured that the market would soon go into a tail spin. Friends and associates attempted to stay his action, but without success. The market moved upward to the surprise but not to the disconcertion of the cautious executive. He had never assumed that he could foretell the collapse to the exact day and hour; yet he had no doubt that it was approaching. Pessimists have a way of spoiling the fun and are therefore frequently subjected to the exhortations of the more optimistic.

So it was in 1928. The sanguine brought forward evidence to prove that fears were unwarranted. Clearly, if future earnings were discounted, the prices of most securities were not inflated. The skeptic remained unconvinced. He had known bull markets in the past and he had known their end; he had no reason to believe that the past would not repeat itself. Weeks turned into months, still the reversal did not come. Just the opposite, security prices continued to advance. Slowly, the skeptic lost faith in his own skepticism. Perhaps the past would not repeat itself; perhaps the country had really entered a New Era. The sales and profits of his own corporation had never before been so large, and other concerns with which he was

INTRODUCTION

well acquainted were also breaking records. In July, 1929, he reentered the market with gusto.

When the executive had sold his stock, he had not anticipated leaving his cash uninvested long. One must buy today and sell tomorrow and make a profit in between, for such is the *raison d'être* of business. This much is certain, that unless one buys and unless one sells, one will never make a profit. But immediate pressures are not solely determinative; their potentialities must first be evaluated. Attitudes are all-important, for they prescribe the criteria to be applied. Now attitudes are seldom, if ever, the creation of the moment; their gestation is always prolonged.

The merchandising executive had been in business for several decades and his attitudes were influenced, at least in part, by his earlier experience. He remembered the rich man's panic at the opening of the century, the crisis of 1907, the hysteria at the outbreak of the war, the severe liquidation of 1920-21. In short, his skepticism of 1928 was forcefully conditioned by personal history. While life continues, attitudes remain in flux: a changing reality possesses the ability to modify them. This is the more true if the changes be substantial and of longer duration. The expansion of the economy between 1922 and 1928 was not sufficient to eradicate completely the executive's memories of earlier days, when upon occasion depression rather than prosperity was the leitmotiv. Yet the additional nine months of startling advances, reinforced by the power of mass suggestion, were sufficient to alter his attitude. Clearly, his conversion was difficult; the majority were molded and remolded more easily.

3

THE ILLUSION OF ECONOMIC STABILITY

One need but recall that in the winter of 1928-29 a large industrial corporation located in the Middle West investigated the possibilities of opening a branch factory in the South. Its business below the Mason and Dixon line had grown rapidly, but profits had failed to keep pace. The more favorable location of competitors necessitated the absorption of large freight costs. Upon investigation, a suitable site was discovered. The company decided upon expansion even though it realized that in the immediate future such a move, by increasing its total capacity, would adversely affect manufacturing costs in the North. The Southern unit was opened in the fall of 1929.

This program of expansion illustrates once again the interactions of present pressures and future prospects. It offered the corporation opportunity to improve its competitive position in a new market, and a corporation like an individual cannot afford to let opportunities slip. Yet the ability to reduce distribution costs could not, of itself, have forced the decision. The directors explicitly made important deductions about the trend of business. In reviewing the twenties, they discovered that the South had become an increasingly important customer, and they had full confidence that the trend would continue. Further, they anticipated that the level of activity throughout the economy would be maintained. This conclusion was reached in the face of an interesting case history, for the corporation had opened a branch factory on the west coast just in time for the depression of 1920-21.

The New Era may have been unique in that the overwhelming majority of capable businessmen and powerful corporations were unable to distinguish between the apparent and the real; but if difference there be between the twenties and periods preceding and succeeding, it is solely one of degree. As long as our only approach to the future is through attitudes from the past, mistakes will be inevitable. For instance, during the early days of the depression, President Hoover, confident that the expansion of the twenties would shortly be renewed, persuaded the utilities to quicken capital expenditures on the theory that this action would hasten the return of good times.

The New Deal can likewise be offered in evidence. When President Roosevelt commenced to spend money that he did not possess, most of the financial community cried out from the depths of their unconscious that the arrival of the Day of Judgment could not long be delayed. Unbalancing the budget was not a unique experience, for it had occurred on a large scale during the World War. It had then been camouflaged by hysteria; the depression, however, was no sanction for the destruction of the sacred.

If only the simple-minded were subject to major errors in evaluating the trends of the market, their miscalculations could be ignored. But this is hardly the case. The man of affairs and the student of society improve but slightly upon the analyses of the unsuccessful and the unlettered. The New Era presents the most striking instance. In the early spring of 1929, a group of men distinguished in statecraft, industry, and science completed a detailed survey of the postwar developments in American economic life. Their report concludes in crescendo: "Our situation is fortunate, our momentum is remarkable."

THE ILLUSION OF ECONOMIC STABILITY

The disentanglement of illusion from reality is no simple matter, for ideas, true and false, help to shape the facts just as the facts in turn largely condition ideas. In personal life, the difficulties of correct analysis dog us to the grave. Only death permits us to escape from a struggle in which we are the certain losers, but from which we cannot retire—not even in defeat. In communal life, we are likewise the victims of fate. The past alone affords guidance, yet the future is always different from the past. Err we must.

To discern the counterpoint between the course of business and the attitudes of the business community during the New Era, the Depression, and the New Deal is the object of the chapters that follow. Since economic stability was the boast of the twenties and since economic stability has been the elusive goal of the thirties, its history is crucial for an understanding of our economy.

A cursory review of the industrial development of the country between the Civil War and the World War reveals an expansion as intense as it was cumulative, for though the seventies and the nineties knew serious depressions, years of distress were outnumbered by years of satisfaction and elation. Out of a strong tradition of business optimism was born the illusion of economic stability.

In studying the growth of the illusion during the early twenties, special consideration is afforded a group of concerns that sought to eradicate fluctuations in their production and employment. Although tangent to the major story, the study of these experiments throws into high relief powerful forces, typical not only of this small segment but also of the economy at large.

INTRODUCTION

To appreciate the maturity of the illusion necessitates a review of the striking changes in the postwar condition of the laboring class. In addition, the behavior of prices, costs, and profits must be assessed, for these were trusted signposts. Nor can the New Era be evaluated without considering the role of credit and capital.

Although the collapse of the stock market in October, 1929, brought expansion to a dramatic halt, the New Era lived on to influence the course of the Depression and the New Deal. Able to withstand the radical liquidation of the early thirties, the doctrines of economic stability guided President Roosevelt in his intensified search for the promised land.

Encouraged by the prewar trend, the striking advances of the twenties were certain to engender a belief that economic stability had been achieved. But the last decade presents incontrovertible evidence that the belief is illusory. Neither private enterprise nor governmental action has been able to insure the full and efficient utilization of men and machines.

The moral is clear. At all times, the level of business activity reflects past estimates of present conditions and present estimates of future conditions. It has long been recognized that anticipations of the future are largely determined by past performance. Less obvious is the fact that since experience must be interpreted, and since all interpretations contain error, estimates of the future are always faulty. Until men become robots and markets become machines, the economy will be shaped by rational calculations of irrational calculators.

Part One

BIRTH OF THE ILLUSION

CHAPTER I

THE TRADITION OF BUSINESS OPTIMISM

THE nineteen twenties were years of intense economic activity. The record shows the rapid multiplication of houses and automobiles, of radios and refrigerators. Even though this was not the first time in the country's history that activity had been rampant, the twenties were called the New Era. To appreciate the new it is essential to recall the old.

In the past, every period of economic prosperity ran its course and was followed by a depression more or less severe, during which profits were replaced by losses and high wages by unemployment. During the twenties, especially toward the end of the decade, the conviction became widespread that the prevailing prosperity could long continue. This, in face of a widespread recognition that agriculture, bituminous coal, lumber, cotton goods, and several other industries left much to be desired. Depressions were perhaps a thing of the past. The economy was in balance; it could long remain thus.

Today it is clear that the contemporary evaluation of the twenties was fundamentally incorrect, but it is not clear why contemporaries held firmly to the belief in economic balance. The prosperity of the period was respon-

11

sible for much of the optimism, but the populace must have been favorably predisposed to the gospel of enduring prosperity, for seven years are too few to alter fundamental attitudes.

If predisposition there was, it must have been deeply ingrained, for the opening of the decade contributed little to its vitality. The depression of 1920-21 was the most rapid liquidation in the entire history of the country. But only a few years thereafter, the lettered and unlettered sang hosannas to the New Era, an era smug and happy because it felt convinced that depressions were a thing of the past. The emergence and dominance of this pervasive optimism possess a history as interesting as it is obscure. Yet we have a clue. Ideas are frequently reflections of the facts, recognizable if imperfect reflections. Because attitudes are always long in the making, attention must be directed to the trend of economic development during the decades preceding the twenties.

Although industry is only a segment of our economy, the economic history of modern America is, above all, the story of an industrial expansion. True, not until the census of 1920 did the majority of the people reside in urban centers, that is, in places with a population of more than 2,500; and as late as 1930, slightly less than half lived in towns with more than 8,000 inhabitants. Despite the predominance of rural factors in earlier decades, despite their marked strength today, it nevertheless remains true that the most accelerated changes were typical of the industrial-urban rather than the agricultural-rural sectors of the economy. Since cumulative tendencies are our particular interest, the picture will not be skewed badly if we concentrate upon the growing rather than the declining, the dynamic rather than the static.

Although the industrialization of the economy was greatly accelerated by the Civil War, a thorough review of the transition from farm to factory could not stop short of the earliest period of colonial history. For a story in which the action takes place in the twentieth century, a background inclusive of the Civil War will suffice.

During the four years of civil strife, the more typical manifestations of a governmentally engendered boom were present; the demand for almost every commodity was insatiable, though purchases were made with money fresh from the printing press. Prices more than doubled, a process that contributed greatly to the creation of new fortunes; though prices stopped rising after the cessation of hostilities, the economy readjusted rapidly and then renewed its advance propelled, above all, by the phenomenal expansion of the railroads.[1]

In the late summer of 1873, a small railroad went into bankruptcy and shortly thereafter the important banking firm of Jay Cooke and Company was forced to close its doors; an expansion of long duration was brought to an abrupt halt. Large wages and large profits quickly gave way to the unemployment of men and capital. Bad times took a big toll in commerce and industry; the sufferings of unemployed urbanites and price-shock agriculturalists swelled the total. Until 1878, conditions remained more or less unsatisfactory, though the five years of strain were relieved, if not released, by fortuitous factors. Many unemployed still possessed intimate contacts with the farm where they could return to eat, to sleep, and to await the revival. Further, industry was in its infancy. Though several branches were severely stricken—the production of pig iron and rails dropped more than 25 per cent—others were able to rise against the trend. For instance, in 1873, steel production totaled 200,000 long tons; in 1875, 400,000; in 1877, 600,000. The emergence of new industries aided in keeping the depression within bounds.[2]

Not until the last two years of the decade did conditions take a marked turn for the better; but once recovery set in, it grew rapidly. Within six years, railroad mileage in operation increased 50 per cent, coal production more than 100 per cent, the value of building permits 150 per cent. The advance, however, was arrested in 1884-85. The statistics of the recession illustrate beyond a doubt that the disturbance was not so severe as that of the preceding decade. The rate of increase in the physical volume of production declined rapidly, but there were few absolute reductions. Yet trouble was caused by the failure of the annual rate of increase to maintain itself. A well-informed observer estimated that in 1885 more than a million men were unemployed and 13 per cent of the factories in the country were either partially or completely shut down. Once again, the trek to the Pacific through fertile plains and rich forests proved highly advantageous. During the poor year 1884, six western railroads carried a tonnage 33 per cent in excess of that transported during the prosperous year 1881.[3]

As 1885 was left behind, the expansion again set in, not

to be interrupted until eight years later. The middle nineties proved difficult, perhaps the most difficult since the Civil War. During the quarter-century cumulative changes had occurred, changes that enhanced the dangers of a depression and made escape more difficult. Industrialization had proceeded apace; the quantity of capital invested in industry had increased fivefold and the number of wage earners had doubled. Large overhead costs increased the vulnerability of industry to sudden shrinkages in demand. For the most part, urban laborers had lost their contacts with the farm, thereby complicating the problem of relief. In 1895, two thirds of the cities in Massachusetts were forced to create work projects for the unemployed. The frontier had almost disappeared and industry was no longer in its infancy. Above all, the railroads that had done so much to color the preceding decades had now entered a new stage. Between 1883 and 1893 railroad mileage in operation increased 40 per cent; during the following decade the rate of increase was only half as large.[4]

Bad times in industry are always more serious than bad times in agriculture, for idle men and idle machines cannot feed themselves. A pecuniary-technological system performs wonders when it is working smoothly, but once the machine runs into difficulties its principal assets become liabilities. So it was in the nineties when the economy contracted rapidly. For the first time, informed observers began to question what until then had been beyond the pale of intelligent discussion, whether the entire economic structure could survive. Confidence was shaken,

THE ILLUSION OF ECONOMIC STABILITY

if not undermined.* In fact, one sector of the economy had begun to worry long before the depression got under way and had taken measures to reassure itself. The agreements and combinations between competing concerns typified by pools, trusts, and mergers were conditioned as much by fears of large losses in a shrinking market as they were stimulated by prospects of large profits in an expanding market. But in 1897, the economy took a turn for the better, and before the century had run its course, the country was in the midst of a new and substantial prosperity.[5]

During the three decades following the Civil War, the economy suffered three marked reverses: the middle seventies (1873-77), the middle eighties (1884-86), and the middle nineties (1893-96). This reckoning suggests that years of prosperity were three times more common than years of depression. Experts have made, however, a much more pessimistic appraisal of the period, 1865-1900, one that finds only nine tenths of a year of prosperity per year of depression. This conclusion cannot be lightly dismissed but it may well be questioned.†

* Professor E. R. A. Seligman recalls a conversation with Jacob H. Schiff of Kuhn, Loeb and Co. in which the failure of a renewed expansion was seriously discussed. It was Mr. Schiff's belief, however, that the world demand for our lumber, agricultural products, and minerals would insure, irrespective of domestic factors, a strong revival.

† Although Thorp and Mitchell emphasize the inevitable limitations of *Business Annals*, the following comments are perhaps in place: the materials upon which the annals are based have a strong bias in favor of financial transactions; the categories "recession" and "depression" are applied even if the declining trend is modest and of short duration; between 1873 and 1900, fourteen years are designated as depressed but particular mention of unemployment is made in only five years (1873-74, 1884, 1894, 1896) and in only three years (1873, 1894, and 1896) is attention called to severe or widespread unemployment.

16

THE TRADITION OF BUSINESS OPTIMISM

In 1889, David Wells, one of the most astute observers of the American scene, in a book entitled *Recent Economic Changes* reviewed the major economic developments throughout the world during the years 1873-89. Wells begins his analysis by reflecting upon the unprecedented disturbance and depression in trade, commerce, and industry—phenomena that first manifested themselves in 1873 and persisted with fluctuating intensity up to the time of writing. The author remarks that this observation is common to all informed persons. After four hundred and more pages of detailed analyses, he arrives at a group of interesting conclusions. The period under review has been for mankind movement upward, not downward; for better, not for worse—this epoch will hereafter rank in history as one without parallel: the world commands a more comfortable subsistence than ever before; the dawn of the day when poverty will be abolished is not far distant. The contradiction between Wells' introduction and conclusion is perhaps more apparent than real. Frequently, prosperity is identified with rapid increases in the price level, for changes in conventional markings may bring with them mirages of great wealth. The Civil War was such a period. During the following decades the price level tended downward; the interruptions to the decline were minor and without significance. The opportunity to earn profits is probably diminished by difficulties engendered through falling prices: contractual obligations can only be slowly readjusted; inventory losses must frequently be suffered; new investments are discouraged. Wells' dichotomy can now be understood: the wartime

17

inflation was a thing of the past, as were the phenomenal profits typical of that era. In comparison, business activity during the seventies and the eighties was depressed—but only if depression be measured in terms of the rising prices and paper profits of the Civil War. If more significant criteria be applied—the employment of men, the investment of capital, the physical volume of production, the standard of living of the masses—Wells' panegyric was in order. Nor can one doubt that his was the opinion of the majority.[6]

Since the publication of Wells' book was followed by the depression of the nineties, investigation is in order to determine whether the economic misfortunes of that period diminished, or perhaps destroyed, the optimistic tradition of earlier years. During the depression, questions were raised, but the reappearance of prosperity in 1896 answered them.

In 1902 was published the *Final Report of the Industrial Commission* based upon nineteen volumes replete with data, factual and interpretative. It was an unparalleled record of American economic development during the nineteenth century. A cursory survey permits only one conclusion: the Commission was greatly impressed with the economic progress of the country. The depression of the nineties was remembered and those of earlier decades were not forgotten, but the periods of stress had been too few and far between to affect the basic finding that the industrialization of the economy had been a boon to all.[7]

The rapid expansion of the industrial sector of the

18

economy during the last thirty years of the nineteenth century could not fail to establish a tradition of business optimism; any other reaction would have been abnormal. The occasional interruptions, typified by empty factories and unemployed men, must have proved disturbing, but they were so infrequent as to upset only the most sensitive. The history of immigration confirms this analysis. Between the end of the Civil War and the close of the century no fewer than fourteen million people immigrated to the United States. Economic conditions in their respective native lands were improving, yet they chose to come to a country strange in language and in custom. If the movements are studied in detail, a simplified pattern emerges: a cessation in the rate of growth of the American economy such as occurred in the middle of each of the three decades was followed by a radical reduction in the number of new arrivals, usually in excess of 50 per cent from the previous maximum. After a few years, when the economy again began to expand, new records were established. The peoples of Europe reacted similarly to the people of America: each had great faith in the future of the United States, a faith that wavered slightly when subjected to the strain of depression but was renewed and intensified as soon as expansion again occurred.[8]

If the economic developments during the latter part of the nineteenth century instilled an optimistic bias into the business community, the behavior of the economy during the first decade and a half of the twentieth century helped to reinforce this disposition. After falling for more than thirty years, the price level suddenly reversed itself in

19

1897 to start a climb that it maintained for many years. The impetus to business from a slow but steady price rise cannot be overlooked. The bondholder may suffer, but entrepreneurs are greatly encouraged. A conservative appraisal of the years 1896-1915—the latter date marks our economic, if not our political entrance into the war— discloses a ratio of three years of prosperity per year of depression, a striking improvement when compared to the ratio for the latter decades of the nineteenth century. Aside from minor difficulties in 1903-04, business was substantially good during the years 1898-1907. In the latter year, a financial panic occurred. Sudden and severe, it had repercussions less serious than one would at first have anticipated. In 1908, the physical volume of pro- duction was only 6 per cent below that of 1907, only 7 per cent below that of 1906. Surely, a small decline. Its significance is even further diminished when one recalls that the volume of production for the depression year 1908 exceeded that of 1901 by 25 per cent and that of 1903 by 8 per cent, though 1901 and 1903 were, accord- ing to the records, years of better than average output.[9]

With the rapid subsidence of the banking panic of 1907, the expansion of the economy was renewed. By 1913, the total volume of production was 50 per cent greater than it had been at the beginning of the century; wage earners in manufacturing industries increased during the decade following 1899 by about 2 million or more than 40 per cent; the quantity of capital invested in manufacturing doubled (from 9 billion to 18 billion dollars). Allowance for large increases in population would substantially reduce, but would not cancel, progress measured on a per capita basis. Despite the fact that in the years following the panic of 1907 dividend disbursements indicate a heightened profitability of industry, doubt remains whether this period surpasses the opening years of the century.[10]

In a rapidly changing economy, man can only dream of situations so stable that everybody is employed and everybody is making money. Stress and strain are of the essence of change. To estimate their magnitude is, however, no easy matter. Unemployment is perhaps the most significant criterion, for the balance between the supply and demand for productive forces, especially labor, has been recognized as the most fundamental of all adjustments. During the first fifteen years of the century, employment in manufacturing shows between the peak of a boom and the trough of a depression only one annual decline in excess of 10 per cent. Though the distress began to be relieved at the end of nine months, the financial panic of 1907 was sufficiently disturbing to force the figure up to 15 per cent. At the outbreak of the war, conditions were unfavorable; indicative thereof is the fact that unemployment remained for some time in the neighborhood of 10 per cent. Nor was it until the early months of 1915, when the Allied Powers entered the American market on a large scale, that the economic system recuperated rapidly.[11]

During the first decade and a half of the twentieth century, then, the rapid growth of the economy was interrupted once—toward the end of 1907—and was slowed up once—prior to the outbreak of the World War. The era was marked by a high degree of stability: prices rose slowly but steadily; markets continued to expand; prolonged depressions similar to those of the seventies or the nineties were conspicuously absent. Business was carried on under circumstances as favorable as they were stable, though economic discontent and social conflict were not absent. If general optimism had been the natural consequence of the economic development of the latter years of the old century, rampant optimism seemed justified by the performance of the economic system during the opening years of the new century. The worst scourge of industrial capitalism was absent: serious depressions belonged to history. The future held only promise.

For five years (1915-20) the economy was so directly influenced by the European massacre that the period has a story of its own. During hostilities, substantial advances occurred: the physical volume of manufactured goods increased 40 per cent; the number of persons engaged in manufacturing increased by more than 30 per cent; the net income of corporations for the year 1915-16 was twice that of the preceding twelve months, and 1916-17 proved as profitable as 1915-16. During these years, the demands of business and government for accommodation led to large increases in the money supply: between 1914 and 1918 total deposits of all banks increased 45 per cent and by 1920 they had doubled. The unusual behavior of prices, wages, and profits was closely associated with these financial manipulations. If bonds were no longer emitted, or even if they were turned out more slowly, serious repercussions could not be avoided. Increases in the money supply worked havoc with established institutions and attitudes; only veterans of the Civil War could orient themselves.[12]

With the cessation of hostilities in November, 1918, business immediately became hesitant. No oracle was needed to warn that major readjustments were a necessary accompaniment of transforming a war to a peace economy. The Armistice brought uncertainty; but before many months had passed, the expansion was renewed with vigor. When at the end of twenty months it finally collapsed, the community was taken unawares, for its fears had been dissipated amidst a profusion of profits.

The breadth and intensity of the depression can be gauged by the fact that during the twelve months following June, 1920, the level of wholesale prices dropped 35 per cent. Profits tumbled more rapidly; corporate net income for 1921 was more than 90 per cent below that of 1919. If the labor situation is reviewed, the magnitude of the upheaval becomes even more vivid: unemployment in 1921 was estimated at 4 million; of the men who had been employed at the height of the boom, one out of seven was in the streets.[13]

Economics deals with relatives, not absolutes. Hence, to assess the postwar collapse, one must restudy prior depressions. The data are extremely inadequate, but it appears that the *percentage* of the laboring force unemployed during 1920-21 was twice that of the nineties, and the *number* of unemployed twice that of 1907. The rapid industrialization of the economy during the first two decades of the twentieth century, evidenced in part by the doubling in the number of employees attached to manufacturing industries, adds significance to the magnitude of unemployment during the postwar depression. If certain alleviating factors were overlooked, its severity would be unique. It is, however, important to remember that the large profits and high wages of the war years ensured that losses would not always precipitate bankruptcies and unemployment would not always presage destitution.[14]

The influence of the depression upon prevailing attitudes was slight. Not until the late summer of 1921 was the federal government forced to take cognizance of the economy's disruption. The approach of winter led President Harding, at the suggestion of Secretary Hoover, to summon a conference on unemployment. One hundred leaders of industry, labor, and the public met in Washington during the last days of September for the interchange of opinion and formulation of policy.

In their addresses of welcome, President Harding and Secretary Hoover emphasized that the prevailing disruption was clearly an inheritance from the war. The President advanced the belief that the twenty months of business expansion which followed the cessation of hostilities were more elation than restoration; in his opinion, a severe depression was inevitable. He feared, however, that the already excessive unemployment would further increase. Mr. Hoover was more blunt. Either the unemployed would again be put to work or else the entire moral and economic system might collapse. The preceding winter had not proved taxing because labor was still in possession of substantial savings, but these were now exhausted. If the liquidation were to continue, the future was indeed ominous.[15]

Fifteen thousand enterprises had already been forced into bankruptcy and many more were operating at severe losses. But the Federal Reserve System had prevented the depression from degenerating into a panic; further, the decline in the physical volume of production did not exceed 17 per cent; finally, construction was expanding. Conditions were bad but far from hopeless. Industrialists pointed out that once the gap between their costs of production and their selling prices was narrowed business would again expand. Representatives of agriculture pointed out that the ratio of prices paid by farmers for goods bought to the prices received from goods sold had dropped 25 per cent within the last year. Clearly, recovery awaited a readjustment of prices: in August, 1921, beef cattle brought the producer only 90 per cent of the 1913 price; in the same month wages in meat-packing plants were 85 per cent above 1913, freight rates on dressed meats had increased by more than 210 per cent, and retail prices had risen between 10 and 60 per cent. The major complaint was directed against the high remuneration of labor, for wages had risen more than 100 per cent during the war and postwar years. Much of the increase had been neutralized by advances in selling prices, but the impression persisted that a readjustment of wages would precipitate an expansion of industrial activity. So argued the employers; not so Mr. Gompers.

He fought every reduction on the ground that such action would impair the purchasing power of the largest group of consumers, thereby defeating the very purpose at which it was aimed.[10]

Acute awareness of the many difficulties, buttressed by fear of the European situation, did little to stimulate among the well-informed optimism about the immediate future. The Conference estimated, however, that a tremendous expansion in construction was not unlikely—the estimate ran as high as twenty billion dollars—which if it developed would contribute greatly to a new period of prosperity. If taxes were kept within reason, recovery would probably not long be delayed.

The business forecasts for 1922 evince a high degree of uncertainty, in part a reflection of the fact that the changes wrought by the war had demolished the trustworthiness of the criteria of old. But not even the gloomiest surrendered his fundamental optimism. Recovery might be slow, but recovery there would be. Prosperity was foreordained; history was its guarantor.[17]

The rapidity of the revival that set in at the beginning of 1922 startled even the optimists. By the end of 1921, the declines in prices and production had, for the most part, been arrested. To contemporary observers the sudden reversal of the trend proved confusing and the passage of time has perhaps decreased but has not eliminated the difficulties of explanation. Economic expansion is a function of two variables: the availability of unused resources, especially men and capital, and the existence of prospects sufficiently enticing to insure their utilization. In retrospect, it appears that in 1922 the economy possessed both. Men there were aplenty and money was ample. In several branches of the economy, investment of capital was almost mandatory. Applied science had been greatly stimulated by the war, but industry, except in a minority, had not been directly affected by this technological advance. During hostilities, effort was directed toward increasing output; replacements and improvements were postponed. During the postwar boom, fantastic advances in prices, following the initial uncertainty, resulted in further delays. Once it became clear that the depression would not be turned into a rout, and that labor would strenuously resist wage reductions, the incentive to install new equipment was strengthened. The production of capital goods rose markedly during the two years, 1921-23: the output of rolling mills more than doubled; cast-iron pipe increased in like amount; machinery and transportation equipment jumped 45 per cent within twelve months.[18]

The technological progress of the automobile industry, in addition to the transformation of its selling activities— the installment plan was radically expanded—led to a substantial spurt in production. During the years 1921-23 output was doubled. This advance was not without influence upon the closely allied industries of rubber tires and petroleum; they likewise underwent a marked expansion.[19]

Most important was the behavior of construction. Since the outbreak of the war, the annual volume of construction had failed, with only one exception (1916), to equal that of 1913. At the end of the war, the cumulative shortage forced the passage of rent-restriction laws that the courts hesitated to invalidate. At the President's Conference on Unemployment, the conviction was widespread that with readjustment of labor and material costs the building trades would rapidly expand so that before long two million men would be reemployed. At the time of the Conference, the index of building costs stood at 150 of the 1913 base, having declined from a high of 310 in March, 1920. Charges for financing were likewise high; but despite these and other impediments, the volume of new construction for 1922 was 50 per cent in excess of the preceding year, 35 per cent greater than 1913.[20]

Once the fantastic prices of the postwar boom were reduced to recognizable levels, entrepreneurs began to utilize the unused resources of men and capital in order to satisfy the latent demand for houses and automobiles. The influx of European gold relieved the banking system of strain and the rising income of agriculture proved helpful. As 1922 drew to a close, the war was fast receding. A new era was dawning.

Part Two

GROWTH OF THE ILLUSION

CHAPTER II

THE STABILIZATION OF THE INDIVIDUAL CONCERN

INDUSTRIAL capitalism has developed to a hitherto unparalleled degree the institutions of technology and money. During the decades preceding the outbreak of the World War, the economy became ever more dependent on the requirements of these institutions, but circumstances obscured the full extent of their control. With the exception of the serious depression of the nineties, the country had been remarkably free from the worst scourge of modern industrialism—prolonged unemployment of men and machines. Absence of epidemic was interpreted as evidence of immunity; but the reverse was perhaps the more true, for changes in the environment were heightening the potential virulence of infection.

The severe liquidation of 1920-21 might well have served as a warning that the creator was becoming the victim of his own creation. The sudden shrinkages in demand that necessitated the shutdown of large plants and the precipitous unemployment of millions, who depended upon the possession of money for the purchase of their daily necessities, were facts so unpleasant that they could not be overlooked. Reality can, upon occasion, break through the protective crust of optimism. Yet the implications of the depression were for the most part disregarded. The unsettlement of the economy was ascribed to an extraneous factor—the war.* Yet a recurrence of the prevailing distress was not feared, at least not at once, for a review of the country's history indicated that a half-century or more had passed between one major war and another. Conviction was widespread that the prewar trends toward economic stability would once again assert themselves. Though faith alone might have sufficed, silent factories and sullen men placed a premium upon action.

In fact, contemporary belief in the quick return and lasting permanence of economic prosperity was based upon action of an earlier day. During the decades of intense industrial expansion, the financial system had occasionally given way—especially in 1907. Monetary disturbances then could not always be isolated; unemployment and bankruptcies frequently followed in their wake. Consequently, the establishment of the Federal Reserve System in 1914 was hailed as insurance against recurring panics. The first years of the System's existence helped to transform that anticipation into actuality. Seldom had the country been subjected to financial strain comparable to that of the war, yet the System worked well. Never had the country been forced to undergo a

---

* "The Great War of 1914-18 produced an economic cataclysm that enmeshed almost every human being in the civilized world. There will be no dissent from the statement that the world has not yet passed out of its shadow. It seems to me to be highly dangerous to convey any impression that the United States in 1921 simply passed through the depression of an ordinary business cycle." Prefatory Note by Walter R. Ingalls to *Business Cycles and Unemployment*, New York, 1923.

liquidation so sudden and severe as that of 1920-21, yet the System cushioned the decline. Toward the end of 1921, Secretary Hoover pointed out that although the business community had always considered the cyclic financial panic as inevitable "we know now that we have cured it through the Federal Reserve System." Encomia for the System were in order; faith in the economy was warranted. Surely, if the trend toward economic stability had been able to make substantial headway during the prewar years when the banking structure had suffered from weak underpinnings, it could easily be accelerated now that successful repairs had been completed.[1]

Freed from the fear that the behavior of money and credit might at some future date upset a restored balance of the economy—the Federal Reserve System had been tried and proved—the business community directed its attention to the ways and means whereby this restoration might more readily be achieved. Even if the prevailing optimism about the avoidance of serious depression in the future had not been widespread, the prevailing mores prevented a direct attack upon cyclical fluctuations. A strong tradition of individualism placed almost insurmountable obstacles in the path of political control over the instabilities of business enterprise. Economic diseases of epidemic proportions could not easily be attacked by a therapy grounded in individualism. Interest and ability aside, the most powerful corporation was unable to influence the general course of business; at best, it could only partially avoid the dictates of the trend.

Faith in the potentialities of central banking to pre-

vent the emergence of unsettling factors combined with
the taboo against multiplying the techniques of social control. Vulnerable to the instabilities of a laissez-faire economy, the business community could not act. Inhibited
from dealing with cyclical fluctuations, leaders of industry
sought comfort in their optimism. But action was still
possible. The wide-scale unemployment of men and machines typical of a depression had its counterpart in
seasonal oscillations. True, the economic and social implications of monthly fluctuations were frequently so different in degree that they could hardly be equated in kind.
Yet there were many and striking similarities. Seasonal
irregularities in production and employment resulted, not
unlike cyclical disturbances, in the idleness of machinery
and men. The depression of 1920-21 threw into high relief the costs involved in the partial utilization of economic resources. To industry, idle machinery was a serious
liability; to labor, idle days were a curse. The infrequency
of serious depressions heightened the importance of seasonal fluctuations. It was estimated that year in and year
out the clothing worker, the shoe worker, the building-
trades worker, and many others were idle about a third
of their working hours. Despite compensatory factors of
higher hourly wages and perhaps a longer working day,
the losses occasioned by seasonal unemployment were by
no means eradicated.[2]

Seasonal irregularities were surely as old as the industrial system, probably as old as the oldest economic system. It is scarcely surprising that businessmen, limited to
a theoretic interest in cyclical instabilities yet desirous of

participating in the regularization of economic activity, turned their attention to seasonal fluctuations. Individual entrepreneurs could attack the problem; socialized action was not a prerequisite. The taboo against interference did not apply. History lent encouragement, for the prewar efforts to reduce and control seasonal fluctuations in production and employment had not turned out badly.[3]

The depression of 1920-21, by precipitating interest in the problems of overhead costs and unemployment, suggested in no subtle manner that a reduced periodicity in employment and production would prove profitable. Moreover, the scientific management of industry, a movement known to the prewar economy but much expanded under the pressures of wartime production, emphasized the wastefulness of irregular employment. Increasingly, managers realized that the frequent hiring and firing of men was costly, for in many industries a laborer reached average efficiency only after several months of steady employment. Studies of labor turnover indicated that the costs of hiring a single man frequently ran as high as several hundred dollars.[4]

Morals contributed a mite to the stabilization movement. Despite the impersonality—some have called it the soullessness—of capitalistic production, instincts other than the acquisitive have not always been atrophied. In fact, phenomenal success in business frequently dissolves merely pecuniary aggressiveness. Captains of industry not infrequently become benefactors of the arts and sciences. A few join the ranks of social reformers. In spite of unavoidable concern with wage rates and productivity—a competitive economy punishes the inefficient with extinction—social experiments are not completely outlawed. A paternalistic interest in the health and happiness of one's employees has scope for expression this side of outright philanthropy. Above all, if the will exists the fetters of custom may be broken and experimental ventures fostered. The many years of prosperity during the opening decade of the century, climaxed by the phenomenal profits of the war, laid the groundwork for paternalistic ventures.

The spurt of interest in the regularization of industry, typical of the first years of the twenties, may be satisfactorily explained by the factors already outlined: the fears of instability engendered by the depression of 1920-21; the scientific management of industry which concentrated upon the economical utilization of men and materials; the desire of paternalistic employers to improve the lot of their laboring forces by eliminating the unfortunate consequences of irregular employment. But these factors, or their counterpart, were present in the days before the war; hence it is questionable whether they offer a complete explanation. *A priori*, the impress of the war should be investigated. More likely than not, the wartime alterations in social and economic conditions aided the stabilization movement.

For more than a century the gospel of laissez-faire had been preached from the mountaintops and, tariff legislation excepted, the deviations from the true faith were few and far between. Each innovation was a direct challenge to the orthodox who prophesied that heresy would be rewarded by confusion and chaos. The World War broke the taboos; the government was forced to assume control over many sectors of the economy. With the passage of every month, the controls became more stringent. Yet the economy did not collapse; in fact, it continued to operate with a considerable degree of efficiency.

Until the outbreak of hostilities, experiments in the state control and operation of economic institutions were kept at a minimum; the doctrine of noninterference was strongly entrenched. The short interlude of the war broke the monopoly of laissez-faire. The enthusiastic support by the business community of the "back to normalcy" drive was well founded, for only the speedy cessation of social experimentation could save vestiges of the taboos against state interference with economic life.* The frequent disparagement of governmental efforts was a premeditated attack upon group action and an implicit defense of the individualism of old. The attack was well grounded, for as the more intelligent men of affairs so clearly perceived, conscription helped to shift the emphasis from the individual to the group, a shift that could not fail to enhance the power of the masses. Emancipated from taboos and possessed of the vote, the masses might secure from the legislatures that which they could not win in the market place. For instance, it was no longer certain that

* The recent departures from orthodox governmental financing that began under President Hoover and were intensified under President Roosevelt can perhaps be in part explained by our experience during the war and immediate postwar period. With the exception of the short depression of 1920-21, the economy responded favorably to radical increases in the national debt. Moreover, it was possible during the twenties to make sizable reductions in the total and to carry the remainder without difficulty.

industry could escape responsibility for the excrescences of industrialism and at the same time feel assured that the state would not interfere. The belief in political incompetency having been in part exploded, recourse to government appeared imminent.[5]

The changing role of the state and, more important, the fears of its continuing metamorphosis doubtless contributed much to the stabilization movement. If incentives for collective action could only be dispelled, individualistic methods might have a chance of survival. Clearly, to remedy by private endeavors much, if not all, unemployment would go far to forestall the adoption of social controls. The incidence of the war upon the masses was not limited to this shift in matters political; economic relations were directly affected. During the four years 1916-20, trade-union membership increased 80 per cent; as the many strikes at the end of the war so clearly illustrated, labor knew how to use the bargaining power thus enhanced. With the adoption of the new immigration policy, it became clear that labor would have to be handled more circumspectly.[6]

This strengthened position of labor was probably the most important consideration in interesting far-sighted employers to experiment with the control of seasonal fluctuations. Clearly, steady employment would be an efficacious bar to unionization and a good guarantee for a contented labor force. The depression of 1920-21 with its widespread unemployment of men and capital focused attention upon the evils of instability. The President's Unemployment Conference of 1921 applied the spur. "They [the employers] returned to their plants and began an effort to stabilize employment in their industries. They obtained some success and then more and as they succeeded and realized what they had gained, they became missionaries in the field."[7]

The dictatorship of the weather in agriculture and the tyranny of custom in trade ensured that experiments in the control of seasonal fluctuations would center in manufacturing. One must harvest in late summer; Christmas cards cannot be sold after December; but an assembly line can operate throughout the year. Moreover, the accelerated mechanization of industry promised substantial rewards for the more efficient utilization of equipment. But the risks of innovation limited the number of experimenters: in general, only dominant corporations ventured to pioneer.

Seasonal fluctuations could be attacked either by readjusting the annual volume of production and employment or by enlarging the total. Adjustments in daily or weekly hours of work to harmonize with periods of active and slack business afforded the most direct means of reducing fluctuations in employment. If products had different seasonal peaks, the same objective could be achieved by training a labor force to work on more than one specialty.

A complete program of stabilization was, however, concerned not only with eradicating fluctuations in employment but also with eliminating the wastes of idle equipment. Favorite among the more inclusive techniques was production for stock. Whenever production was limited

by expensive machinery, a skilled labor supply, and
highly seasonal sales—as in the case of Eastman Kodak—
manufacturing in advance of sales was mandatory. Warehousing was usually limited to standard products or parts,
but even style-ridden industries like men's clothing, neck-
ties, and hats were not completely beyond the pale.[8]

Production for stock was a trusted experimental technique; a sample of 69 companies showed that 41 followed
the practice of accumulating inventory during lulls in selling. Many corporations were, however, unable or unwilling to assume the entire burden of stabilization; they
preferred to divide both costs and profits. Although irregularities in production and employment would persist
as long as consumers played favorites with the months,
the majority of manufacturers dealt with middlemen
rather than with consumers. True, the distributive trades
were forced to guide themselves by the actions of consumers, but they nevertheless retained considerable latitude.
To shift the burden of seasonality to trade, manufacturers offered discounts for early ordering; occasionally,
the discount would be disguised in the form of future
dating of early orders. If products were difficult to store,
concessions were contingent upon early shipment.[9]

Price adjustments and price protection played important roles in the stabilization movement. Although Eastman Kodak did not grant discounts for early orders, it
was willing to make sizable allowances for returned merchandise. Several concerns, among them Procter and
Gamble, protected important customers from general price
reductions. In the Mazda Lamp Division of General Elec-

tric the problem did not arise, for all merchandise was sold on consignment.*

Variations in the hours of work, production for stock, and price manipulations sought to eliminate seasonal fluctuations through leveling the peaks and filling the troughs. By increasing the annual volume of business and using the increases to fill in the troughs, the same result could be achieved. This alternative found favor with many. Powerful advertising campaigns enabled Coca-Cola and B.V.D. to turn seasonal into yearly products. The canning industry, which was severely handicapped by the irregular flow of its raw materials, made substantial progress by increasing its line of merchandise. Supplementary products, though typical of the food industry, were used successfully by manufacturers of paper, optical goods, clothing, and machinery.[10]

The addition of a filler or two did not always suffice; more radical programs were occasionally necessary. Direct control over selling suggested itself. In order to secure a steady market for advance orders, Knox Hat acquired seventy retail stores; Endicott-Johnson and Melville Shoe likewise looked with favor upon the ownership of distributive outlets. When Procter and Gamble first became interested in stabilization, it vastly increased its direct selling to retailers in order to eliminate the speculative purchasing of jobbers.[11]

* An interesting sidelight on cyclical fluctuations in morality is offered by the consignment system. During the prosperous twenties, practically no jobber falsified his records to delay remittances, but in the midst of the depression approximately 20 per cent jockeyed their accounts in order to increase their working capital.

Production for stock, price manipulations, fillers were, however, limited techniques. Only a few weeks of excess production were sufficient to convince an enterprising manufacturer of the hopelessness of warehousing automobiles. Adequate storage facilities were quickly exhausted and the Detroit winter played havoc with the gains from stabilization. Since the depletion of working assets is seldom justified, small concerns feared to tie-up large amounts of working capital in inventory. Stable prices have usually been viewed with favor, especially by the well-established, that sector of industry which was most active in the stabilization movement. Hence, if interpreted as the first move in a general price decline, discounts for early ordering might prove more harmful than beneficial. Only in those rare cases where it was possible to establish a specific scale of discounts for an entire industry could price reductions for early ordering be encouraged. Nor were fillers always certain boons. Upon occasion, they failed to gain a secure place in the competitive market; additional distribution costs might cancel the gains from a more regularized production schedule; they could develop a seasonal shift of their own.

In addition to these technical limitations, the experiments were seriously handicapped by developments in the economy at large. Willingness of merchants to accumulate inventories in advance of selling peaks was the key to successful stabilization but, after the severe price liquidation of 1920-21, hand-to-mouth buying became increasingly popular. Moreover, the substantial heightening of railroad efficiency and the expansion of motorized freight reduced the pressure on dealers to enter into long-time agreements with their sources of supply. In 1927, Secretary Hoover estimated that improvements in the railroad system had facilitated a reduction of 600 million dollars in the normal inventories of retail lumber dealers. The more widespread use of cost analysis convinced many merchants of the dependence of profits upon turnover, a discovery that militated against the holding of large inventories. In short, the marked trend toward close buying was a major obstacle in the path of stabilizing manufacturing operations. During the twenties, excess capacity in industry was the partial reciprocal of lessened inventories in distribution.[12]

More detrimental was the growing importance of style. The standardization of products had been stimulated by the experience of the war, yet the twenties witnessed marked inroads of style in producer-goods as well as consumer-goods industries. Even mammoth generators were beautified. International Shoe and Endicott-Johnson, the largest shoe concerns in the country, bemoaned the fact that the trend away from staples greatly increased the difficulties of regularizing employment. Changes in style were not always whimsical variations introduced by aggressive producers; frequently they evidenced marked improvements in quality. Yet 14,000 variations in the different models of a medium-priced car, and the impossibility of prejudging the specific novelties that would please the consuming public, illustrated the necessity of a cautious inventory policy.[13]

As the twenties progressed, the number of industries

immune from the vagaries of the novel declined rapidly. Men's clothing lost its conservatism; watch chains were no longer staid; mail-order catalogues, the outpost of the drab, offered kitchen sinks in a variety of colors. In the middle twenties, conservative Eastman Kodak, a close rival of conservative Mr. Ford in its predilection for the color black, began to market vanity kodaks in all the colors of the rainbow. The experiment failed, but cameras soon appeared in futuristic designs. Increases in the production of semiluxury and luxury articles, with their inevitable emphasis upon style, were the natural concomitant of the general expansion of the economy. Moreover, manufacturers, realizing that women controlled the purse strings, paid particular attention to form and color. Since gains from regularized production were seldom sufficiently great to outweigh the dangers of a stagnant inventory, style became the *pons asinorum* of the stabilization movement.[14]

In face of these multiple obstacles, experiments to reduce seasonal fluctuations were venturesome and the success of the experiments was remarkable. As the New Era approached its climax, the Senate Committee on Education and Labor held protracted hearings on Unemployment in the United States, at which time the leaders of the stabilization movement were afforded ample opportunity to testify. That the experimenters made a marked impression upon the Committee can be gauged from the summary of its expert:[15]

The significant thing about the regularization of employment and the elimination of seasonal variations is the fact that wherever it has been tried it has been found highly profitable. Without exception every business executive who testified before your committee stated that the regularization of employment had brought with it decreasing costs per unit of product.

The eradication of seasonal fluctuations frequently led to reductions in the costs of labor, overhead, and distribution. The ability to offer regular employment made it possible for successful experimenters to pay wages slightly below the competitive level; and though the majority failed to exploit this advantage, they secured important benefits. The best workers gravitated toward the reliable concerns. Moreover, steady employment was an important safeguard against the deliberate restriction of output, a weapon as valuable to labor as it was costly to capital. The eradication of peaks and troughs in production resulted in a more efficient utilization of investment; if machinery were very expensive and the product easy to store, as with Kodak, large savings in overhead costs proved possible. The addition of fillers facilitated declines in distribution costs per unit of product; a salesman could usually sell five articles as easily as he could four.[16]

These gains from stabilization were directly dependent upon trends in the economy at large. Between 1922 and 1929 the wholesale level of prices remained remarkably stable, and the serious risks attendant upon fluctuating prices were thus at a minimum. Since every experiment in the eradication of seasonal fluctuations necessitated planning, the absence of untoward disturbances reduced the possibilities of miscalculation. During the New Era, in the second place, production and profits increased rapidly. To fill in seasonal troughs by enlarging production was comparatively easy, especially when large profits offered a convenient source of capital with which to finance the experiments. Finally, under the impetus of general expansion the price of labor tended to rise, establishing a premium on all innovations that succeeded in reducing labor costs.

The pecuniary aspects of the stabilization movement, though highly important, were not paramount, for as the movement gained strength its social implications were pushed to the fore. Stabilization was the answer to the class struggle: careful experimentation could increase profits for the manufacturer and at the same time free labor from the costs of unemployment. When Senator Walsh of Massachusetts queried Mr. Daniel Willard as to whether self-interest or altruism was the motive behind stabilization, he was told: "Partly each." During the course of the Senate hearings, a leader in the movement explained that "Yankee ingenuity and Yankee imagination" formed the partnership that directed this specifically American attack upon the instabilities of modern industrialism.[17]

The enthusiastic missionaries prophesied that, once employers recognized its value, the habit of stabilizing would be incorporated into business practice just as filing, typewriting, and specialty salesmen had made their way. Mr. Willard opined, and in this judgment he was joined by Mr. Lubin, the expert of the Senate committee, that stabilization could most easily be promoted by a state of mind. The enthusiasts repeatedly emphasized that the movement was in complete harmony with the best traditions of American business and in no way ran counter to its basic motivation—individual initiative.[18]

Philosophy is experience rationalized. The metaphysics of the stabilization movement must be explained by the success of the experimenters in regularizing employment. Procter and Gamble found it possible to guarantee 48 weeks' employment in the year; Hickey-Freeman reported that its cutting department had worked full time for a period of four years; Bethlehem Steel was able to show minimal fluctuations in payroll. This achievement was not merely a by-product of the stabilization movement. From the start, the eradication of fluctuations in employment had been a major objective; hence this phase of the experiment was subjected to the most careful analysis. Industry, in regularizing employment, had succeeded in increasing the annual real wages of its employees and had thereby enlarged the demand for its products. Larger volume led to lower unit costs, which in turn led to larger total profits. The cycle was complete.[19]

During the nineteen twenties, business expanded so rapidly and so steadily that fears of a reversal were almost completely stilled. If profits alleviated anxiety, they did not eliminate thought. Theory alone could master the facts. Although only a small group of concerns deliberately experimented with the stabilization of their operations, the success that they achieved led them to ascribe the greatest importance to their efforts. Above all, they were convinced that the regularization of employment was largely responsible for their well-being. The economy at large was likewise wallowing in prosperity, a condition most frequently explained by the improved status of labor. High wages were the key to salvation.

Time proved that the prosperity was ephemeral. Yet the heart of the illusion—of both the stabilization of the individual concern and of the stabilization of the economy —must be sought in the doctrine of high wages.

Part Three

MATURITY OF THE ILLUSION

CHAPTER III

THE DOCTRINE OF HIGH WAGES

DESPITE the conspicuous ignorance of Europe about American conditions, on one point it has long been well informed. Foreigners have known that American wages are unique. As early as 1776, Adam Smith speculated on the markedly superior position of the colonial laborer and concluded that the explanation must lie in the youthfulness of the American economy. Smith anticipated that once the colonies outgrew their infancy the discrepancy in wages between old England and new America would tend to disappear. Smith was an astute observer, for he prophesied that the center of English civilization might some day shift from London to New York; but in his speculation about wages he erred, for the differential still exists.

In the struggles over the tariff, information about comparative labor costs was widely disseminated. At the beginning of the nineteenth century advocates of free trade emphasized that the fostering of new industries would endanger the high wages of American labor, for the cost of living would inevitably be raised by the tariff. Later the protectionists appropriated the high-wage doctrine. If foreign manufacturers were permitted freely to sell their wares produced under conditions of lower labor costs,

American industrialists would be forced to lower wages and thus endanger the American standard of living. Failure to limit competition could result only in the bankruptcy of American industry and the unemployment of American labor. In the welter of propaganda about tariffs, no doctrine proved more important than this; even today, it retains a potency out of proportion to its age.[1]

Toward the end of the nineteenth century, American industries exported increasing quantities of semimanufactured and manufactured products, a fact of great importance in helping the country emerge from the severe depression of the nineties. With the passage of years, the trend was accelerated: in 1901, the total value of exports was 1,300 million dollars, of which 500 million dollars was in semimanufactured and manufactured goods; in 1913, total exports had risen to 2,300 million dollars, of which manufactured articles comprised 1,100 million dollars. Clearly, high-wage rates did not prove insurmountable.[2]

Before the turn of the century, the question had been raised whether high wages could in any respect be considered a liability. Were they not more boon than bane? American industry was primarily concerned with the domestic market, and high wages ensured a public with ample purchasing power. True, competition abroad might be handicapped; but since the conquest of foreign markets depended not upon low wages but rather upon low labor costs, the payment of high wages was not fatal. High efficiency and high wages might result in low labor costs, a likely contention when one recalls the proverbial efficiency of American industry.[3]

THE DOCTRINE OF HIGH WAGES

The high-wage doctrine so popular during the New Era had a long and chaotic career. Money wages after the World War were appreciably higher than those that had prevailed in the decades preceding the war, a fact that led many to correlate the rise in wages with the general expansion of the economy. The doctrine of high wages sought to establish a causal relation between the two. Since the fancies of the twenties were in part based upon the facts of preceding decades, the latter must be reviewed if the former are to be appreciated.

Between the opening of the century and the outbreak of the war, the economy developed rapidly.* If dividends on common stock be indicative, these were prosperous years. The gains, however, were not shared equally. The average real earnings of employed workers increased less than one half of one per cent per annum; large sectors of the working class actually suffered losses. Wage earners in manufacturing, clerical and low salaried workers, government employees secured increases in money wages, but these increases were smaller than the rise in prices. However, a marked extension in free services for schooling, health, and recreation prevented a reduction in their standard of living. Further, the general expansion of the econ-

* A leading industrialist privately expressed the view that the most effective attack upon the prevailing low level of economic activity would be a radical revision of our immigration policy. In his opinion, the constant stream of new arrivals that characterized our economy in earlier days, made three major contributions: first, industry was protected against any prolonged period of excess capacity; second, since immigrants were willing to accept a standard of living below that of native workers, the latter received considerable psychological gratification; third, a highly fluid working population was the best safeguard against an aggressive labor movement.

omy facilitated the escape of many from the ranks of labor to those of entrepreneurs. Immigrants filled the gap. Even so, during the first decade and a half of the twentieth century, the members of the laboring class advanced but few rungs in the long climb toward comfort and security.[4]

The changes wrought by the World War were more spectacular than substantial. Although the average annual earnings of all employees (excluding farm labor) rose from approximately 700 dollars in 1914 to 1,100 dollars in 1918 and 1,500 dollars in 1920, real earnings advanced but slightly. The rise in prices was so rapid that the laboring man was only 4 per cent better off in 1918 than he had been in 1914, and in 1920 his total gains did not exceed 6 per cent. Once again, the available figures do not tell the entire story. In our society, family income is the key to consumption. During the war, the number of members per family engaged in industry underwent a marked rise, a fact that helped to lift the standard of living of the masses.[5]

Despite the upward trend of wages between 1914 and 1918, that resulted in an average gain of about 8 per cent in the real annual earnings of labor in manufacturing industries, the war was not an unmixed blessing. Small declines in real annual earnings were suffered in agricultural implements, leather goods, and motor vehicles; losses of 10 to 14 per cent were registered in paper and printing, lumber planing mills, and butter and cheese. Precipitous was the decline in the earnings of clerical and salaried workers, for their contracts could be revised only with difficulty; the real earnings of governmental employees dropped as much as 25 per cent. Most striking was a loss of 29 per cent in the real earnings of telephone and telegraph employees.[6]

The armistice in France was a prelude to war in Pittsburgh. Despite the large number of strikes during the intense postwar boom, labor made small gains. In midsummer of 1920, the turbulent expansion came to a sudden and dramatic end; within twelve months the wholesale level of prices dropped in excess of 35 per cent. Production was curtailed and the ranks of the unemployed swelled until 4 million men were out of work.[7]

The depression wrought marked changes in the fortunes of the employed and unemployed alike. Between September, 1920, and July, 1922, hourly earnings in manufacturing industries declined more than 20 per cent. Since hourly earnings are usually a function of two variables—wage rates and output—and since output per worker has a tendency to increase during periods of severe unemployment, the reduction in wage rates must have been considerable. However, real hourly earnings increased during the first half of 1921, for the decline in prices was more precipitous than that in wages; during the latter half of the year, the reverse process set in. Not until the beginning of 1923 did real hourly wages reach their predepression level.[8]

The experience of "union" and "nonunion" wages must be differentiated. During the war, patriotism, by contributing to the social ostracism of the strikers, succeeded in holding organized labor in check; as late as 1920 the real hourly earnings of union labor were below those that had prevailed at the beginning of the war. The depression helped to tip the scales. So successful was the resistance of organized labor to reductions in wage rates that real hourly earnings increased approximately 25 per cent.[9]

As the depression began to lift, the outlines of important gains were discernible; by the end of 1923, the markings were clear. During the three years 1920-23, the real annual earnings of all employed laborers increased 15 per cent, an advance of marked significance when one recalls that during the thirty years following 1890 the total gain had been only 10 per cent.[10]

The recovery of the early twenties followed a unique pattern, for, though hourly earnings jumped 15 per cent between the middle of 1922 and the end of 1923, the general level of prices advanced but slightly. To explain this conjuncture is not easy. Recourse can be had to the startling advances in the productivity of labor; in 1922, output per person increased 20 per cent. The reappearance of profits at a time when hourly earnings were rising and selling prices were remaining more or less stable can doubtless be in part explained by increases in the productivity of labor; more important, they reflected the reemployment of unused resources with the concomitant rise in the total volume of production.[11]

The severity of the price decline during the early days of the depression of 1920-21 gave ample indication that the wartime level of wages and prices was doomed to rapid revision, and in a desperate effort to get its bearings the business community reviewed the prewar scene. In July,

1914, the average hourly wage of all employees in manufacturing industries was slightly under 25 cents, whence
it rose to 60 cents at the height of the postwar boom. Of
course, this increase in money wages went hand in hand
with a decrease in the purchasing power of the dollar, so
that labor improved its position but slightly. But the depression inaugurated an appreciation in the value of the
dollar, thereby arousing the greatest concern about the
high level of money wages. With wage rates 150 per cent
above 1914, the scope for contraction was indeed great.
Under pressure of the general decline in business activity,
hourly earnings dropped 25 per cent within two years.[12]

If industry had taken full advantage of the prevailing
economic stress, there is reason to believe that the decline
in wages would have been considerably larger. However,
powerful employers had strong incentives to proceed circumspectly. Unionism, after making most substantial
gains, had only recently been stopped in its tracks. The
struggle against outside organization had been greatly
aided by the adoption of welfare programs whose efficacy
would have been greatly reduced if wage rates were radically readjusted.[13]

After adopting a modest program of wage reduction,
many entrepreneurs developed misgivings about slowing
down if not arresting the decline in wages. Perhaps the
price for industrial peace was too high. At the President's
Unemployment Conference of 1921 the opinion was commonly voiced that business recovery hinged upon a radical readjustment of the price structure; above all, upon
large reductions in the price of labor. Failing this, recov-

ery might be endlessly delayed. Yet recovery set in despite the failure of prices, wages, and costs to decline to their prewar level. Nor was the momentum of the recovery seriously impeded in 1922 and 1923, even though the hourly earnings of labor advanced markedly.[14]

The occurrence of the unexpected proved as disturbing as it was pleasant. The forebodings of the business community had obviously been unwarranted. At the outset of the depression Henry Ford had pointed out that reductions in wages would prove a boomerang by reducing the purchasing power of the masses. The majority of employers, however, paid scant attention to the harangues of the Dearborn eccentric. They went their way reducing costs by reducing wages, increasingly worried by their slow progress in achieving a thorough liquidation. To their great surprise, the advance of the economy took place before their goal had even been sighted. Their logic having been found wanting, a new logic was in order. Nor was it long awaited. As early as 1923, Secretary Hoover emphasized that a return to normalcy did not imply a return to prewar levels. The rise of 10 to 15 per cent in the productivity of labor illustrated the necessity of a new and higher base. The President of the United States Chamber of Commerce gave expression to similar sentiments. The course of events recalled Mr. Ford's panegyric on the virtues of high wages, for the passage of every day proved more clearly that economic recovery and the postwar level of wages were not incompatible. Shortly, high wages were viewed as the cause of business expansion, an interpretation already implicit in the original formulation of Mr.

Ford. By the middle twenties, commentators at home and abroad turned the implicit into the explicit.[15]

In the fall of 1925, Professor Thomas Nixon Carver of Harvard University published a book entitled *The Present Economic Revolution in the United States;* the first of the false prophets had begun to preach. The author believed that the collapse of the Hohenzollerns and the rise of the Bolsheviks were minor events when compared with the contemporary developments in American industry. High wages accomplished much; industrial relations were beatific, prosperity was being widely diffused, the economic system was approaching a state of balance. The majority of students paid slight attention to Professor Carver's analysis; his supporters were mostly observers from abroad. In the same month that he published his findings, a group of German trade unionists arrived in the United States for a short visit, during which they hoped to appraise the postwar developments in American economic life. Their conclusions were later made public.

In sum, the Germans ascribed the greatest importance to the advanced technology of American industry. The prevailing prosperity, they held, must be explained in terms of the efficiency of the industrial machine rather than the fortunate combination of rich natural resources and a relatively sparse population. They were, however, not unaware of the shortcomings of a prosperity that forced one third of the industrial employees of the country to live in poverty—annual income below 1,100 dollars; that permitted only four industries to pay a fair minimum—1,600-1,700 dollars; that enabled the employees of no industry to enjoy a cultural minimum—2,000-2,500 dollars. Yet the commission emphasized that the real annual earnings of American laborers were almost 350 per cent in excess of those in Germany. To explain the marked difference in the productivity of the American and German economies, the trade-unionists alighted upon the doctrine of high wages. Industrial capitalism had long suffered from an inability to sell the goods that it was capable of producing. In America, captains of industry were willing to admit that high wages were the cause rather than the result of prosperity; hence, they were no longer inhibited from enhancing the purchasing power of the masses. The authors of the report explained the expansion of the twenties in terms of the new wage policy of American industry. They felt assured that European, in particular German, employers stood to gain greatly by the adoption of this enlightened attitude.[16]

Englishmen were also impressed by "The American Economic Wonder." After a short visit to the United States in the fall of 1925, two British engineers published the results of their survey in a small volume entitled *The Secret of High Wages*. A hasty review of the developments since 1922 led them to pay particular attention to the increasing spread between wages and selling prices. In seeking to explain the rise in real wages, the engineers laid great stress upon the rate of technological innovation and its stimulating effect upon the productivity of labor. Selling prices could be reduced while wages were being increased. The British complimented the business community upon its acute awareness of the value of high wages for the maintenance of prosperity; but unlike the German investigators, they did not consider high wages the cause of the expansion. To them, the liberal remuneration of American laborers bespoke a high level of industrial efficiency; the machine was responsible for the well-being of the economy in general and of labor in particular. But on one point the investigators of both countries agreed: Europe could gain greatly by following in the footsteps of America.[17]

In 1925, the fortunate position of the economy was more obvious to strangers from abroad than to trained observers at home. True, since the autumn of 1921, the economy had been on the upgrade; but the trend had been interrupted in 1924, at which time unemployment increased, the physical volume of production dropped 3 per cent, and the net income of corporations declined 8 per cent. Measured from the high level of 1923, a year of intense economic activity, the declines were not serious. Yet the retardation in the rate of growth and the absolute declines were sufficient to forestall a rampant optimism, especially in view of the fact that the most strategic industry in the country—automobiles—suffered a decline of 10 per cent.[18]

As 1924 was left behind, expansion resumed: years of intense activity followed one upon the other; only 1927 left something to be desired. Increasingly, the enthusiasm of Europeans found its counterpart among domestic observers. The United States was in the throes of an economic revolution; the diagnosis had been confirmed and, what is more, there was increasing agreement as to etiology. The high-wage doctrine of prosperity was commonly accepted. Evidence of the improved position of the working class was so plentiful that only a cynic could have doubted the strategic role of high wages in the expansion of the economy.

Superficial observation revealed that the majority of the population was enjoying a standard of living unparalleled in the annals of the country. Between 1922 and 1928, the number of passenger cars in operation increased from 10 to 20 million; the number of radio sets increased a hundredfold—60,000 to 6,500,000; the number of homes possessing standing bathtubs increased 50 per cent; the installation of telephones mounted by 60 per cent; homes wired for electricity almost doubled. In part, these advances reflected enhanced expenditures of the wealthy and middle classes, but their magnitude indicated the participation of at least the upper strata of the laboring class.[19]

Between 1923 and 1927, the total number of employed persons increased about 9 per cent and the total wages paid out by industry mounted by no less than 15 per cent. Total family income rather than the earnings of the individual worker is the best clue to the position of labor, and total family income was rising during the twenties at the same time that the average number of dependents per family was declining. The substantial rise in the standard of living of the masses—a trend that became increasingly clear after 1925—was conspicuously influenced by the decline in the prices of luxury goods, above all, of automobiles, radios, electrical appliances, and the like. No longer was the possession of these articles limited to the well-to-do; prosperity was being diffused throughout the land.[20]

In addition, the doctrine of high wages received support from the fact that during the decade many successful employers introduced unemployment and pension plans that indirectly increased the real earnings of labor. Further, employees were frequently afforded opportunities to buy company stock at less than the market price. Nor can the changing status of labor be fully appreciated unless one recalls that a minority of wage earners were able to enter the ranks of salaried employees, a group that made marked gains during the twenties.

This galaxy of facts gave the doctrine of high wages considerable support, but more important than the facts were the encomia showered upon the doctrine by labor and capital alike. Criticism can seldom withstand enthusiasm, for enthusiasm is always strongly motivated.

As early as 1923, the business community, cognizant that recovery was on its way, was less intent upon reducing the postwar scale of wages. Unpleasant, in fact dangerous, the lifting of the depression made the task no longer essential. As the recovery gained momentum, employers became increasingly conciliatory. The liquidators of yesterday affirmed their allegiance to the doctrine of high wages. In truth, a revolutionary change, yet one which, for all of its idealistic trimmings, was grounded in pragmatism. For years without end, the toiling masses had striven to secure a larger share of the product of their labor, a struggle in which they had been fought every inch of the way. Though the weapons had changed, the struggle continued throughout the New Era. The high-wage doctrine was used by employers to prove that labor was receiving the highest possible wage; since prosperity depended upon high wages, any other policy would have been foolhardy. Labor drew different conclusions. If the doctrine were sound, it followed that the more wages were raised, the more prosperous the country would be. By scrapping its earlier wage theories, that had centered upon increases in money wages and latterly upon increases in real wages, labor sought to strengthen its claims by adopting the productivity theory of wages. It was common knowledge that the productivity of labor was rapidly advancing, and labor contended that wage rates should be increased in light of these advances.[21]

Supported by plausible evidence from the workaday world, inflated by the attention paid it by labor and capital, heralded by intellectual sycophants as the key to utopia, the high-wage doctrine came and conquered. Had the doctrine not pretended beyond statistical summary, fault could not have been found. At the end of the New Era, wage rates and total annual earnings were assuredly larger than they had been at the beginning of the twenties; they were markedly larger than those that had prevailed in the decade before the war; they were incomparably larger than those known abroad. But the doctrine made no such modest claim; it was not satisfied with a simple tautology: the American workman receives the highest real wage in the world equals the American workman has the highest standard of living in the world. Prop of the economy, Atlas demanded respect.

THE DOCTRINE OF HIGH WAGES

No longer was it assumed that wages reflected economic conditions; they determined economic conditions. This epoch-making shift in wage policy was independent of any fundamental alteration in the attitudes of the participants. As always, employers were interested in maximizing their profits and wage earners were desirous of enhancing their earnings. Yet the contention was abroad that captains of industry were now willing to pay high wages (really higher wages), for they stood to gain by such action. Even if these high wages would in the first instance deplete the working capital or surplus of a corporation they need not be withheld, for shortly after disbursement they would reappear in an enhanced demand for goods. The increased purchasing power of labor would not express itself in a demand for imported china, rare books, or hand-carved furniture but rather for articles produced under conditions of large-scale manufacturing—automobiles, household appliances, radios, and the like. Afforded an opportunity to reduce his unit costs, a manufacturer could increase his profits as long as his unit selling prices fell somewhat more slowly than his total unit costs. But even a retarded reduction in selling prices would still further stimulate sales, thereby initiating another cycle of lower costs and larger profits. As long as the majority of the population were inadequately supplied with goods produced under conditions of decreasing costs, there were no serious limitations to this harmonious interplay of higher wages, increased demand, lower unit costs, lower selling prices, larger profits. True, the process of reducing costs was not without danger, for upon occasion, it might be achieved through the displacement of men. If the displacement were cumulative, the benefits would indeed prove ephemeral. Technological progress had been proceeding apace for more than a hundred years, yet total employment had never been so large. For instance, a steel company upon introducing a labor-saving device might be forced to dismiss several men; before long, lowered costs would lead to lower selling prices. Automobile manufacturers capable of purchasing their raw materials more cheaply would probably drop their selling prices. Soon, the demand for automobiles would increase, thereby enabling the automobile and steel industries to expand. The unemployed steel worker could then be reabsorbed, perhaps in his old company.

The argument from history was impressive; even more impressive were contemporary economic trends. During the latter twenties, total production expanded rapidly, total labor income increased appreciably, and total profits mounted steadily. In the search for an explanation, the high-wage doctrine of prosperity appeared to be a perfect fit. In harmony with the prevailing optimistic bias, the doctrine escaped careful analysis. Only a cynic distrusts the pleasant, yet a review of the statistics and the logic would have melted the cynic's frozen heart.

Between 1923 and 1928, the average hourly earnings of employees in manufacturing industries increased only 6 per cent, their weekly earnings only 2 per cent, and their annual earnings did not advance more than 6 per cent. Since money wages reflected real wages during the twenties, the wage data of this representative group offer slight substantiation of the high-wage doctrine. The wage data of common labor reinforce this story, for workers employed on highway projects received 38 cents an hour in 1923 and 40 cents in 1928. Union labor was, however, more fortunate; between 1923 and 1928 employees in the strongly organized construction industry secured an increase of 25 per cent in hourly earnings. Despite popular belief to the contrary, with the exception of the small sector of unionized labor, hourly earnings advanced but slightly during the New Era. Assuredly, the startling prosperity of the twenties did not depend upon increases of less than one per cent per annum in the hourly earnings of the laboring population.[22]

Nor is the doctrine much strengthened by a review of changes in the distribution of the national income during the twenties. In 1922, the share going to "wages and salaries" was 67.4 of the total and in 1929 it had risen to only 69.2, with the most rapid gains occurring in the salaried group.[23]

Statistics aside, the casuistry of the doctrine should have been patent. Clearly, no employer could afford to pay wages in excess of the market rate on the assumption that such advances would result in an increased demand so large that his total additional receipts would exceed his total additional costs. Since the wages of his employees would be spent primarily on the purchase of articles produced by others, increased wages would inevitably lead to increased costs that would not be compensated by increased receipts. Although the New Era gave rise to many delusions, American industrialists did not suddenly develop suicidal manias.

The widespread acceptance of the doctrine of high wages greatly strengthened the belief in economic stability, the illusion, par excellence, of the twenties. Under the sway of the doctrine, optimism ran rampant; fundamental contradictions were politely denied. The doctrine, founded on faith, could be demolished neither by statistics nor logic. Not even the destruction of the New Era could annihilate it.

CHAPTER IV

SIGNPOSTS OF STABILITY

ONCE the economy recovered from the severe liquidation of 1920-21, production, employment, and
profits expanded rapidly and with few interruptions. As
one good year followed another, observers were intent
upon estimating the permanence of the expansion. Despite a century and more of intensive application, economic theory was of limited utility in the analysis of economic reality. Yet it did proffer aid. Since wages were
not only a major cost to industry but also a major source
of purchasing power, observers were careful to study developments in the labor market. In fact, the doctrine of
high wages had sought to prove that in a changing economy it was possible for real annual earnings to rise, unit
costs to decline, and total dollar profits to mount—simultaneously. Although this doctrine contributed greatly to
the prevailing optimism, prices, costs, and profits were
likewise investigated in the hope that these important signposts would help to chart the economic wilderness.

To discover whether prevailing trends would continue
or not in the near and more distant future was a task of
great difficulty. As previous decades had done, the twenties studied prices carefully. Rentiers would be much affected by the price for money; farmers were enriched or

impoverished by changes in the prices of agricultural commodities; the trend of industrial prices was a major determinant of profits. More important than individual prices were composite indices. Because of its inclusiveness, the index of wholesale prices was placed in a position of priority.

Of necessity, the study of prices was historically conditioned. The past alone could be utilized as a base for measurement and though rapid changes in economic institutions undermined the comparability of the data, especially if comparisons were made with years far distant, this limitation could be recognized but not avoided. During the New Era, anticipations about the future trend of business were greatly influenced by contemporary evaluations of wholesale prices. Only if these analyses be placed in perspective can the conclusions be appreciated.

Usually unstable, the behavior of wholesale prices was conspicuously erratic during the Civil War. In the short space of four years, the index rose in excess of 100 per cent, an advance so unprecedented that it was thoroughly mistrusted. Justly so, for in the first two years after that war, prices declined 20 per cent and thereafter continued to fall, though less rapidly. From the end of the war to the crisis of '73, the decline totaled 35 per cent. With only a slight interruption at the beginning of the eighties, wholesale prices continued to decline until the middle nineties. During these three decades, the total decrease was not less than 65 per cent.[1]

The depression of the seventies was long and severe and that of the nineties was perhaps even more intense. A declining price level was clearly unpropitious. True, rapidly rising prices were likewise no guarantee of economic stability, for the immediate post-bellum period was unsettled. The more moderate rise in prices typical of the early eighties was associated with business prosperity, but one of limited duration.

From the turn of the century to the outbreak of the World War, wholesale prices rose slowly. During this period, the economy was in a good way, for serious depressions were unknown. Beginning in 1915, a feverish advance in wholesale prices set in, not to be reversed until the precipitous collapse of 1920-21. The experience of this period tended to confirm certain correlations between the behavior of wholesale prices and economic activity. Periods of rapidly rising prices were typified by intense economic activity (1860-65; 1915-20), but the expansions would exhaust themselves within a few years and would be followed by hard times. Periods of rapidly falling prices (1920-21) could prove very trying. Moreover, slowly falling prices left something to be desired, for the two severe depressions of the seventies and the nineties occurred while the price level was sagging. Years of slowly rising prices (1879-83; 1898-1915) were years of good business; but the middle eighties knew a minor depression, as did the first decade of the twentieth century. One correlation was perfect: price movements upward or downward, rapid or slow, were in every case associated with, or followed by, periods of more or less intense business depression. Instability in wholesale prices foretold instability in the economy at large.[2]

71

THE ILLUSION OF ECONOMIC STABILITY

Since the World War had wrought havoc with the prevailing structure of prices, the New Era was especially conscious of price movements. In response to the insatiable demand of the government for goods, the index of wholesale prices rose 90 per cent between 1915 and 1918. Because the armistice presaged the withdrawal of the government from the several markets, it was commonly believed that a rapid liquidation of prices would set in. But it did not; after a short period of uncertainty, prices began to climb, and in 1920 they were 20 per cent higher than at the conclusion of the war. This phenomenal spurt, which brought the index to 120 per cent above 1915, led the more optimistic to believe in the permanence of the new level. Hardly had they voiced their opinion when the structure broke. Within twelve months, the index declined about 40 per cent. By 1922, the disruption of prices and production had run its course, and the economy once again began to expand despite the fact that prices were still 40 per cent above 1913.[3]

As the liquidation was left behind, it became increasingly clear that the uninterrupted decline in prices typical of the decades after the Civil War was not likely to repeat itself. Each succeeding year bore proof that the economy had stabilized itself around a new and markedly higher level of prices than that which had prevailed prior to the World War. For seven years, fluctuations above and below the 1922 base did not exceed 7 per cent. These were prosperous years, so prosperous, in fact, that before the end of the decade they were looked upon as unique. Many believed that the prosperity might long endure, a belief

72

that was considerably strengthened by the failure of prices to rise or decline. War prosperity had always been supported by price advances, a fact which insured that prosperity would be as short-lived as the rise in prices. Falling prices were also to be feared, for the most serious depressions in the history of the country occurred during such periods.[4]

Belief in the permanence of the prosperity—the cornerstone of the New Era—was vastly strengthened by price analyses. In former years, the economic system had failed to find peace. Intense activity, typified by large profits and full employment, would be followed by an interlude of reduced demand for capital and labor. Throughout these years, annual fluctuations in wholesale prices were marked, especially if allowance be made for the cumulation of annual changes. The twenties were unique in that large profits and full employment were accompanied by a striking stability of wholesale prices. Confidence derived from history was strengthened by theory. Since the modern economy depends upon the price mechanism for adjustment, failure of prices to vary greatly might suggest the absence of pathological conditions. The behavior of wholesale prices during the twenties invited an optimistic interpretation.[5]

Preoccupation with the index of wholesale prices did not exhaust the exploitation of price data. In the hope of obtaining useful clues to the future trend of business activity, studies were undertaken of the monthly variability and annual dispersions of prices. Once again, the analysis was historically conditioned. During the years from 1896 to 1914, indices of monthly variability and annual dispersion of prices evidenced declining trends. Since this period had been unmarred by serious depression, it was assumed that these declines reflected a heightened stability of the economy. Because of the radical alteration in the price structure during the war and immediate postwar years, the trend was reversed. Once the liquidation of 1921 had been completed, both indices showed renewed declines. Experts were of the opinion that ample justification existed for "considering the developments during the period 1914-21 as so much water under the bridge and for neglecting these in attempting to trace post-war trends." As far as measures of price variability and dispersion were meaningful, comparative studies indicated that the economic system was becoming more stable.[6]

In addition to evaluating carefully the behavior of these general indices, considerable attention was devoted to a study of specific prices. Most important was the price of labor, but other prices were not neglected. Since the crisis of 1907 had been preceded by a steady loss in the purchasing power of farm products, much comfort was derived during 1922-27 from the rise of more than one per cent per annum in the price of farm products. Moreover, this increase was helping to bridge the gap created by the liquidation of 1920-21, at which time the ratio of prices received to prices paid by farmers dropped precipitously: 1913–100; 1920–99; 1921–75. By 1929 the ratio had climbed back to 89.[7]

While the trend in the price of cultivated products was upward, the prices of industrial products declined between

1922 and 1927 at a rate just below one per cent per annum. Experts believed that this rate augured well for the longevity of the prosperity. Once again, historical comparisons were made; between 1902 and 1907 the prices of industrial goods rose at a rate considerably in excess of that for labor and agricultural products. The prewar data evidenced cumulative restrictions in the purchasing power of the bulk of the population, while the New Era witnessed a strengthening in the position of most consumers.[8]

The general decline in the price index of industrial goods must not obscure the fact that during the twenties the prices of many products were subject to infrequent change. This proximate stability was of great solace to the business community and contributed greatly to enhancing its confidence in the future. Intense competition had in the past not infrequently forced market prices to a point so low that they failed to cover overhead costs. The wide-scale development of open-price trade associations during the postwar years indicated the high value that entrepreneurs placed upon stability in their selling prices, especially in a period when unit costs were tending to decline. Despite legal trammels, many industries achieved by convention that which they could not secure by contract. Since instability in prices had always been associated with instability in the economy at large, escape from frequent and substantial fluctuations in prices could not fail to tinge business expectations optimistically.[9]

During the New Era public utilities expanded rapidly, thus further reducing the area in which prices were determined by competition. Since prices subjected to governmental control were highly stable and cost trends were downward, it is small wonder that during this period of expanding business the average annual rate of change in net income was greater in "transportation and other public utilities" than in any other sector of the economy, finance alone excepted.[10]

Although statistical measures are unavailable, there is little doubt that the twenties witnessed a marked expansion of branded and trade-marked articles, a development that increased the role of stable prices in retail markets. Since the search for enlarged markets necessitated increased expenditures for advertising, manufacturers strove to set and maintain a price sufficiently high to cover the overhead costs of distribution.[11]

Historically, fluctuations in the demand for raw materials had always resulted in intensified fluctuations in their prices. During the twenties, the prices of crude rubber, coffee, silk, and sugar were under the special protection of international cartels and national governments. Likewise, copper, nitrates, potash, mercury, and sulphur were treated solicitously. In 1929, the United States began to gamble in basic commodities by financing and warehousing the carryover of wheat and cotton. As the New Era approached its end, only one attempt at valorization had failed completely: crude rubber had escaped its captors. The transient success of these schemes substantially enlarged the sphere of stable prices, thereby contributing to the prevailing buoyancy.[12]

Guided by history and supported by theory, the business community interpreted the price tendencies of the nineteen twenties optimistically. Yet this interpretation was not dictated by the facts. Since increases in the price of labor were likely to affect profits adversely, mistrust of the advances was not completely irrelevant. At a time when the prices of industrial products were declining, increases in the prices of raw materials might eventually cause trouble. Although the individual entrepreneur reveled in the fact that his selling prices changed infrequently, an economy that depended for its adjustments upon the price mechanism could not view this stability sanguinely. Moreover, the elaborate manipulations essential for the control of raw-material prices suggested that eventual failure with dire consequences was not impossible.[13]

In a rapidly changing world, the moral of history and the logic of theory are always limited. Yet they are indispensable, for the critical evaluation of the past offers the sole approach to an intelligent anticipation of the future. To complicate matters, the plethora of data and theories permits of proofs as many as they are contradictory. Selection is fundamental. Small wonder that during a period of marked increases in production, employment, and profits observers sought encouragement from their studies of the past. Desirous that the economy should continue in its present path, the entire community searched for propitious signs. Students of price phenomena, bogged down in data and uncertain of criteria, were greatly influenced by the prevailing optimism. Themselves exposed to the psychology of the era, they optimistically skewed their analytical and historical studies. Unconscious, their optimism was the more powerful.*

Although attention was focused upon the behavior of wages and prices, the paucity of signposts ensured that the trends in costs and profits would not be overlooked. The expansion of the economy depended at long last upon a more efficient utilization of available resources. Costs were the key to efficiency. Hence, the trend of costs was certain to repay careful study in evaluating the prospects of business. Decreases in costs that were reflected in decreases in selling prices offered the most satisfactory mechanism for enlarging production and consumption. Moreover, differentials between costs and selling prices were the key to profits, the alpha and the omega of capitalism.

Between 1923 and 1929 selling prices per unit of manufactured goods declined 9 per cent: during this same period costs of materials and labor per unit of product declined 12 and 14 per cent respectively; overhead costs plus profits increased 5 per cent. Since the combined costs of materials and labor equaled 81 per cent of the total cost of manufactured goods in 1923, the fact that they declined considerably more rapidly than selling prices en-

---

* To contend that price analyses did not permit of unique solution and to contend further that since prices are epiphenomenal it was dangerous, if not false, to rely upon them for a diagnosis of the economy at large— to contend all this and more does not imply that these analyses were irrelevant nor that conclusions drawn therefrom were unwarranted. To view with favor the closing of the gap between the prices of agricultural and manufactured commodities was surely well-founded. Nor can analysts be held responsible for failing to foresee the rampant disorganization that accompanied the latter part of the depression (1931-33). All that transpired after the New Era was not predestined by the New Era!

sured that profits per unit of product were being maintained if not increased. In fact, the more successful manufacturing corporations were able between 1922 and 1929 to increase their profits per unit one and a half per cent per annum. These 1,200 corporations accounted for 85 percent of the total sales of manufacturing corporations.[14]

During the fifteen years preceding the outbreak of the World War, the selling price per unit of manufacturing product increased about one and a half per cent per annum, cost of materials advanced more rapidly, and fabrication costs (labor, overhead, and profits) changed but slightly. If allowance be made for the general rise in prices during this period, the relative position of the several constituents can more easily be analyzed. In sum, the returns to labor and management declined while the suppliers of raw materials used in manufacturing received a larger share. Conditions after the war were vastly different. Though they were forced to reduce their selling prices, manufacturers lowered their costs of materials and labor more rapidly and succeeded thus in protecting their margins.[15]

Clearly, the cost trends in manufacturing during the New Era permitted an optimistic interpretation. By reducing costs, industry found it possible to reduce selling prices, and so to stimulate demand; profit margins per unit of output did not decline, and total profits increased phenomenally. Within the short period of seven years, the more prosperous sector of manufacturing increased its profits from 1,350 million to almost 3 billion dollars. These data might well have precipitated uncertainty about the trend of events, for the gains made by manufacturers hinted at a deterioration in the position of raw-material producers. Industry needs many and prosperous customers.[16]

Nor were savings in labor costs an unmixed blessing. Increases of 18 to 25 per cent in the productivity of labor in manufacturing industries between 1923 and 1929 could have followed only upon substantial additions to physical plant and machinery. Horsepower per wage earner in manufacturing industries increased during the twenties at an unparalleled rate, and production of machine tools increased threefold. Fluidity in capital markets and large surpluses ensured adequate funds for new investments. While the expansion was in process, these outlays more than justified themselves: the spread between total costs and total receipts widened, and overhead costs per unit of product failed to rise. But overhead costs act differently in the short and in the long run. A slackening in the rate of industrial activity would cause serious difficulties. Since the expansion of the economy during the twenties was in part the result of the rapid mechanization of industry, any reduction in the rate of acceleration would depress the capital-goods industries, with unfortunate consequences for the economy at large. Purchasing power released by these industries has always been a potent factor in creating and maintaining a period of industrial prosperity.[17]

As the twenties drew to a close, abatement in technological progress was feared by few. Since 1921, "Americans have found ways of producing more physical goods per hour of labor than before. They have received larger average incomes because they have produced more commodities and services." Reductions in unit costs were still all-powerful. True, the rate of profits during the New Era declined in twenty-eight industries, and the number of commercial failures remained at a high level. But as long as technological improvements continued apace, prosperity was assured. Past experience suggested the possibility of a retardation, but even the cautious student refused to accept experience as a worthy guide. The prevailing optimism had escaped all fetters.[18]

Confidence engendered by the progress of industry was somewhat reduced by the plight of agriculture. The sowers of wheat fared less well than the sellers of bread. For decades, nay for centuries, agriculture had been pushed farther into the background; at the beginning of the twenties, less than 30 per cent of the population continued to live on the farm. Though its decline in power and prestige has been rapid, agriculture remained the most important industry in the country. The preoccupation of Congress with agricultural legislation throughout the twenties indicates that all was not well with the landed interests. Except for the soldier who died in battle, the farmer suffered most severely from the war. At first, everything was jolly: the insatiable demand for the products of the farm ushered in an era of intense prosperity. Of a sudden, it collapsed. The results were dire: capacity was unduly enlarged; debts were burdensome; unit prices were very low. Although the value of farm real estate never recovered during the twenties, the purchas-

81

ing power of farm products increased substantially—almost 20 per cent between 1921 and 1929. From a low of slightly more than 6 billion dollars in 1922, income produced by agriculture varied between 7 and 8 billion dollars during the following years. This rise helped quiet the most serious anxieties about the future of agriculture but it scarcely generated optimism. Encouragement came from another corner.[19]

While the movements of prices during the New Era were working to close the gap between agricultural and industrial products created by the depression of 1920-21, the cost trends in farming promised much. Though readjustments of productive capacity or debt burdens were intensely difficult, reductions in the costs of producing important crops proved feasible. Alleviation, perhaps salvation, loomed on the horizon; mechanization was the savior. During the five years preceding the outbreak of the World War, the number of gasoline tractors manufactured and sold in the United States totaled 30,000. Production spurted during the postwar boom and then declined slightly, only to regain and maintain a level in excess of 100,000 annually throughout the twenties. Harvester-threshers, so important in the new wheat-producing areas, made their first appearance at the end of the war.[20]

When there are many variables, costs frequently hide more than they disclose. Despite serious difficulties, a first approximation to the trend of agricultural costs is not impossible. Average costs depend primarily upon yield, which is largely a function of climate. During the twenties, the total average cost of producing wheat, corn, and oats showed little change; the sample suggests considerable annual variation but no decisive trend. More important than average costs are sample studies of differential costs under varying combinations of factors. Between 1922 and 1929 farmers in the United States bought approximately 4 billion dollars of farm machinery, exclusive of automobiles. Despite the high-pressure salesmanship of agricultural implement companies and the convenience afforded farmers of buying today and paying tomorrow, mechanization was founded upon facts and supported by figures. With wheat selling above one dollar a bushel, the substitution of tractors for horses proved profitable on many, if not all, farms. True, the advantages were limited spatially and temporally, for small holdings could more easily support a horse than a tractor and, if prices fell precipitously, even large holdings would have difficulty in meeting the money costs of mechanized farming. But the differential between the costs of production on horse and tractor farms was so marked during the twenties that mechanization swept the wheat belt. Combines tell the same story. Although the harvesting of 200 acres or less could most efficiently be accomplished by binders and reapers, the introduction of the combine was justified on larger acreage. On farms of 400 acres and more, savings of almost 50 per cent could be secured by the use of combines.[21]

The postwar history of wheat farming is the saga of mechanization. Cotton, the other great cash crop, tells a different tale. During the price decline of 1920-21, cotton dropped within eleven months from 42 cents to 12 cents per pound. The boll weevil then came to the rescue; by December, 1923, cotton was selling at 36 cents per pound. In 1920, the most important of the wheat-producing states reported between 10 and 15 per cent of all farms equipped with tractors; by the end of the New Era the figures had mounted to about 40 per cent. For reasons technological, topographical, and social, mechanization at the beginning of the twenties had scarcely gained a foothold in cotton production; Louisiana alone could boast of more than one per cent tractor farms. Although mechanization increased at a rapid rate during the following years, the absolute figures at the end of the decade were still small; North Carolina, which headed the list, had but 4 per cent mechanized farms. Because of the wide spread between yields on different soils, average costs in cotton reveal even less than in wheat. The data indicate comparative stability in the different categories during the twenties, but costs of production on high- and low-yield lands continued to vary more than 100 per cent. After the war, cotton production moved westward, first to Oklahoma and Texas, and, toward the end of the twenties, to Mississippi and Louisiana. The Atlantic seaboard was losing position rapidly. The new lands invited mechanization: when horses made way for tractors, power costs on a 200 acre cotton farm in Texas were reduced almost 50 per cent. In the wheat belt mechanization probably proceeded beyond the margin of safety, while in cotton production the tractor made slow inroads even in districts clearly suited for its use.[22]

The World War, and more particularly the depression

of 1920-21, presented agriculture with serious if not insoluble problems. The progress of mechanization during the twenties permitted one large group of farmers to escape and held out promise of security to other groups. Clearly some would go under, but that could not be avoided; even the most intense industrial boom could not ensure against losses and bankruptcies. Small farms would be joined together, and the displaced labor would have to migrate to the city. So it happened. But these radical readjustments prevented the farm community from sharing wholeheartedly in the prevailing prosperity. The vociferous farm bloc in Congress reiterated that agriculture was suffering from an emergency, but ten years of wailing turned many sympathizers into skeptics. As the New Era neared its end, agriculture appeared sufficiently well adjusted to ensure, if not to heighten, confidence in the future of the economy. For many farmers, difficult times were ahead; but the opportunity to reduce costs radically guaranteed that general progress would not be impeded by the inefficiency or poverty of the plowman.[23]

Trends in distribution were less propitious. Suspicious that the costs of distribution were mounting rapidly, many feared that reductions in the costs of producing raw and manufactured commodities were not being reflected in selling prices to consumers. Contemporary opinion was much influenced by advertising. In the five years following 1922, the production of motor vehicles increased by approximately one third, while automobile advertisements in periodicals jumped more than 200 per cent. Expenditures for advertising canned foods, tea and cof-

THE ILLUSION OF ECONOMIC STABILITY

fee, candy, and gum showed a twofold and threefold increase during these five years.[24]

With few exceptions, advertising formed a poor index of distribution costs, but more reliable data were frequently not available. A well-informed student of retailing estimated that since the turn of the century the cost of moving goods from the shelves of the store to the home of the consumer followed a slow but steady rise. In 1900, the expense ratio to total sales approximated 20 per cent; by the end of the New Era it was probably 30 per cent.[25]

Trends in retailing can in part be gauged by the efficiency of department stores. Between 1923 and 1928, dollar sales increased about 10 per cent, while the expense ratio in both large and small stores advanced by an equal amount. Additional volume was not accompanied by decreasing unit costs, at least not typically. So far, figures and opinions agree; distribution costs were on the rise. But these data are not exhaustive. The twenties witnessed the most rapid expansion of chain stores, a development that must be carefully reviewed before conclusions are reached.[26]

At the beginning of the decade, the number of chains exceeded 900 with a total ownership of 50,000 stores; by 1928, the number of chains had more than doubled as had the stores under chain management. In 1926, the census of distribution disclosed that in Baltimore, San Francisco, Providence, Atlanta, Chicago, and other important cities chain-store sales amounted to between 20 and 37 per cent of total retail sales. Between 1923 and 1928 the volume of sales mounted rapidly; for instance, wearing apparel and grocery chains increased their dollar volume by 250 to 300 per cent. Of course, sales per store showed no comparable increase: the average per chain store was 12 per cent. Acquisition of old stores and the opening of new stores formed the basis for the expansion. If the most important chains in terms of total volume of sales be selected for study, one discovers that during this period of rapid growth expense ratios did not decline. In fact, between 1922 and 1929 the expense ratio of grocery-store and department-store chains increased 12 and 8 per cent respectively. Dollar-variety, dry-goods, and apparel chains showed a fractional rise, while the trend in grocery and meat and drug chains was indeterminate.[27]

Distribution costs were recalcitrant. Not one of the six important chains could boast of a decline in its expense ratio. In view of the increases in total sales, these rising costs were indeed disappointing. Yet, further analysis shed a little hope. In dry-goods and apparel chains, there was a marked drop in the expense ratio as the number of stores per chain increased: 2 to 5 stores—25 per cent; 100 stores and over—19 per cent. Grocery and meat chains showed a 25 per cent differential in favor of the expense ratios of large chains, and increases in the number of stores led to a declining trend in dollar-variety chains. Even department store chains indicated reductions in the expense ratios for the intermediate groups—100 to 500 stores.[28]

Sound prosperity could only be based upon reductions in real costs, but the twenties proved that cost trends in distribution were mounting. Trends in distribution resembled those in agriculture. Cost per unit of product showed little or no tendency to decline, and frequently the reverse was true. The potentialities inherent in the growth of large chains alone justified a moderate optimism. Just as many farmers would go under while mechanization saved agriculture, so many retailers would be pushed to the wall while large-scale merchandizing increased efficiency in distribution. For the economy at large cost reductions might occasionally prove a drag but never a snag.[29]

If the belief in the stability of the economy was encouraged by the trends of prices and costs, the behavior of profits insured that the doctrine would become dogma. Of all the forces which play upon the stage of industrial capitalism none is more important than profits. Fundamental for the reputation of the New Era were increases in the total volume of dollar profits. Between 1922 and 1929, the net income of all corporations increased from 4,700 to 8,700 million dollars, or more than 7 per cent per annum. The most striking advances were made by corporations engaged in finance and public utilities. The former increased their net income from under 500 to almost 1,200 million dollars, while the latter fared equally well—from 800 to 1,900 million dollars. Nor did manufacturing lag far behind: the net income of all corporations, including those that lost money, showed a gain within seven years of almost 2 billion dollars.[30]

Of course, these averages hide much. In manufacturing, several industries suffered absolute declines in net income; textiles, leather, and lumber knew little of prosperity. The metal, chemical, and food industries were, however, very lucky. But earnings increased in only slightly more than half of the 73 branches of manufacturing; as many as the two fifths of the 90,000 companies finished the prosperous years of the latter twenties with net losses. Yet the decade was prosperous. The proof can be found in the fact that the group which accounted in 1928 for 85 per cent of the total volume of sales of all manufacturing corporations increased its profits from 1,350 million dollars in 1922 to 2,930 million dollars in 1929.[31]

Since farm production is only partially within the orbit of the money economy, significant cash differentials between costs and selling prices cannot readily be established. The changing fortunes of agriculture can be gauged only indirectly. Between 1923 and 1929, the annual income produced by agriculture fluctuated moderately between a low of 7 and a high of 8 billion dollars. Payments for wages and interest as well as withdrawals by entrepreneurs showed great stability. The operating position of farmers can be estimated by deflating gross income from farm production by an index of "prices paid by farmers." On this basis, net income increased during the twenties by almost 10 to 15 per cent, though the steady decline in the value of farm real estate led to a deterioration in total farm equity.[32]

Like agriculture, trade did not keep pace with the profits of industry. In 1922, the net income of all corporations engaged in distribution totaled 695 million dollars, and at the end of the New Era it had risen to only 730 million dollars. While the average annual rate of increase in the net income of all industrial groups between 1922 and 1929 was 7.3 per cent, that for trade showed an actual decline of 0.2 per cent. A study of 664 selected trading companies that remained in business throughout the twenties reinforces this observation. From the end of 1922 to the middle of 1928, this group was able to increase its total net income very slightly: at the beginning of the expansion it equaled a little under 300 million dollars, and at the culmination of the era it had advanced to only a little above 300 million dollars. These figures show that while the industrial sector of the economy was able during the twenties to increase its net income rapidly, agriculture and trade could not keep pace.

Although contemporary observers made this differential diagnosis without difficulty, they met obstacles in evaluating the stability of industry. As always, it was necessary to rely on historical and theoretical analyses. Since the federal income tax was of recent date, figures relating to profits were not available for earlier years. Indirect measures, however, were constructed. Despite serious shortcomings, dividend payments on common stock reflect business earnings. During the years from 1901 to 1913, the cash income, including stock rights, of a representative list of industrial, public utility, and railroad shares increased at a rate of 3 per cent per annum; the capital value of the shares advanced more slowly, a little over 2 per cent per annum.[33]

At the beginning of the recovery from the postwar

liquidation (1922), dividend disbursements to individuals totaled about 2½ billion dollars, while at the end of the expansion the figure was just below 6 billion dollars. The average rate of growth in the cash income, including rights, of a representative list of shares was 16 per cent per annum, and the rate of growth in the capital value was almost 19 per cent. In comparison with the decade before the war, these figures represented increases of 500 and 900 per cent respectively. Not even the years of reduced profits (1924 and 1927) interfered with the rise; for the availability of large surpluses kept dividend payments more or less stable.[34]

The absence of serious depression between the opening of the century and the outbreak of the World War was associated, among other things, with a moderate rate of increase in the earnings of industry. During the second decade, the reverse was true. The striking rise of 100 per cent in dividend payments (1915-17) was followed after a short interlude by the intense liquidation of 1920-21. In estimating the stability of the economy toward the end of the New Era, little comfort was derived from the behavior of profits. Although their rate of increase during the twenties did not equal the record of the war years, it was vastly in excess of that which prevailed before the outbreak of hostilities, an era more useful for comparative evaluations.[35]

Tested by history, the behavior of profits during the twenties gave little support to the optimist. But history was not the only test; theory was also at hand. In estimating the stability of the economy, considerable reliance could be placed upon profit ratios. It had often been contended that a rapid increase in the rate of profits might leave an insufficient quantity of purchasing power in the hands of the masses; that the output of industry not being absorbed, the expansion would come to an end. As the twenties drew to a close, the data indicated that there was little to fear on this score.[36]

Profits measured in terms of capitalization or sales provided typical ratios. In 1922, the capitalization of 3,000 corporations engaged in manufacturing, trade, finance, and mining totaled 22 billion dollars. In that year, net income after payment of the Federal income tax equaled 2,100 million dollars. In 1928, the respective figures were 32 billion dollars capitalization and 3 billion dollars net income. The percentage income to capitalization was strikingly stable throughout the period: the high was 10.2 per cent in 1926; the low, 8.6 per cent in 1924.[37]

If the 2,000 large manufacturing corporations be analyzed in detail, it becomes clear that earnings measured as a percentage of capitalization showed no general increase. In two fifths of the industries profits were definitely declining, while in another two fifths there was no discernible trend; in only one fifth did the rate of earnings increase. The advance was concentrated in producer-goods industries, which had earned but 5 per cent in 1922; while the decline was most general among the highly prosperous group that had earned in 1922 an average return of 15 per cent. For all manufacturing, the fluctuation in net income during the twenties was strikingly small: 11 per cent in 1926 was the high, and the low was reached the following year when only 8.4 per cent was earned.[38]

The relation of earnings to sales has always been looked upon by businessmen as a significant ratio, although the rate of return upon sales varies radically between industries; in meat packing it is customarily below one per cent, while in chemicals it occasionally reaches 30 per cent. The total volume of sales for 2,000 manufacturing corporations increased between 1922 and 1928 from 18 to 28 billion dollars, while net income rose from 1,700 to 2,700 million dollars. Throughout the period, the return on sales hovered around 10 per cent.[39]

If the fortunes of corporations engaged in distribution be evaluated, a substantial but not equal degree of stability in earnings is ascertainable. From 1922 to 1928, 644 trading companies increased their capitalization by slightly less than one billion dollars (1,600 to 2,500 million dollars). During these years, their net income climbed from approximately 250 to 300 million dollars. The rate of earnings on capitalization declined steadily but slowly from 13.5 to 11 per cent. During this same period, sales increased from 4 to 6 billion dollars, while net income to sales equaled 5 per cent. The annual fluctuations were slight.[40]

During the depression of 1920-21, approximately 17 of 106 manufacturing, trading, and mining industries suffered a net loss. In 1928, not a single industry failed to earn a return, although many companies in the several industries lost money. Toward the end of the twenties, two fifths of the 90,000 companies engaged in manufacturing could not avoid the red. About one half, including the two fifths just mentioned, earned less than 5 per cent; nearly one third earned more than 10 per cent; and about one sixth earned in excess of 18 per cent. Despite this striking diversity in the fortunes of the several corporations in manufacturing, the fact remains that throughout the New Era total profits mounted rapidly while profit ratios remained remarkably stable. Increases in net receipts were associated with increases in the total volume of sales and additions to capital investment; but only in a minority of cases did capital investment grow more rapidly than sales, presumptive evidence of future economic difficulty.[41]

The constant and considerable increase in total profits was a function of the general expansion of production. Though the growth of the economy during the twenties affected the profitability of the sectors unevenly, large additions to the total volume of business increased the number of prizes. Contentment with the present, however, did not eliminate concern about the future. Every sign was studied in detail. The trend of prices and costs enhanced the prevailing optimism, and the review of profits further strengthened it. The marked stability of earnings measured as a percentage of either capitalization or sales was interpreted as proof that entrepreneurs were receiving no more than their just returns. Pathological conditions were absent.[42]

In most cultures, preoccupation with the future is the prerogative of a small and select class; the majority exhausts its energy in worshiping the past and practicing in the present. By placing a high premium upon the correct anticipations of future events, industrial capitalism has made prophets of us all. Since divine assistance is reserved for the few, the many are forced to seek aid where they may. In attempting to evaluate, toward the end of the twenties, the trends inherent in the economy, businessmen studied carefully the behavior of prices, costs, and profits. These were the trusted signposts. Theory and history encouraged the placing of favorable interpretations upon small fluctuations in the wholesale level of prices, declining trends in the unit costs of production, stability in profit ratios. The venerable tradition of business optimism led to a compulsive belief in the New Era.

CHAPTER V

THE BANKING MECHANISM

THE World War rehabilitated money in economic analysis, thereby ending an ostracism which had been decreed when Adam Smith successfully assaulted the mercantilist doctrine that the wealth of a nation could be measured by its metallic hoard. Striking changes in bank deposits, governmental debts, and price levels suggested that the influence of money upon the economy at large could no longer be ignored, especially in mature countries such as Great Britain and the United States where financial transactions depended much more upon checks than upon currency. In reviewing the New Era, the banking system dare not be overlooked and the analysis had best begin with gold, the most durable part of the foundation.

In 1920, the gold stock totaled 2½ billion dollars, whence it rose steadily until it reached, in 1924, 4 billion dollars. During the remainder of the decade, its fluctuations were slight. The flexibility of the American banking system depends upon changes in member bank reserves, for deposits based on the loans and investments of member banks—the largest segment of the total means of payment in the entire economy—are directly limited by reserve requirements. The relation between member bank reserves and gold has long been intimate, though not so intimate as the uninitiated might assume. From the beginning of 1922 until the fall of 1929, the net increase in monetary gold amounted to 750 million dollars, a figure approximately equal to the rise in member bank reserves. But this correlation must not be overemphasized. The quantity of money in circulation, the purchase and sale of government bonds, the holdings of eligible paper can likewise influence reserve balances. Since these were subject to frequent change throughout the twenties, the Federal Reserve System was not forced to react automatically to alterations in the gold stock. Yet its latitude was frequently circumscribed. In the last analysis, the expansion of bank deposits during the New Era reflected enlarged demands of borrowers for accommodation, demands that the banking system was able to meet largely because of its increased holdings of gold.[1]

The supply of money consists of two parts: currency in the hands of the public and deposits on the books of the banks. Unequal at the beginning of the twenties, they were even more disparate at the end of the New Era. Between 1922 and 1929, currency in circulation fluctuated around 4½ billion dollars; annual variations were minor and no trend was discernible. Total deposits of all banks amounted to approximately 36 billion dollars in 1922 and 52 billion dollars in 1929. The annals record only one parallel increase, that which occurred during the World War (1914-20). During the war, just as during the New Era, changes in money were associated with striking transformations in the entire economy.[2]

THE ILLUSION OF ECONOMIC STABILITY

Although monetary theory remains the most esoteric field in economics and velocity remains the most esoteric field in monetary theory, no treatment of money can afford to ignore velocity completely. The reason therefor is clear: changes in the rate of turnover of deposits, like changes in the quantity of deposits, can substantially influence the course of prices and production. Between 1922 and 1929, the annual average velocity of demand deposits of New York City banks doubled; and in the case of banks in 140 other cities the average rose by one third. This striking advance in exchange velocity probably reflected, in the first instance, intensified trading in securities, real estate, and speculative commodities, for income velocity which is primarily controlled by changes in the national income, the price level, and consumer spendings showed only minor variations. However, the rise in exchange velocity by directly influencing the prices of financial instruments could not fail, because of the interdependence of all prices, to influence indirectly the entire economy.[3]

As changes in the volume and velocity of bank deposits are reviewed, the monetary history of the twenties unfolds. The story is as simple as it is concrete. Dollars are quantities and changes in quantities permit of measurement. But it must be recalled that new dollars have a habit of coming out of the clouds and old dollars not infrequently evaporate into thin air. Statistics of money shed as much light upon the behavior of the banking mechanism as a census of population reveals about human nature. The increases between 1922 and 1929 of 5 billion dollars in demand deposits and 11 billion dollars in time deposits were associated with marked changes in the portfolios of the banks and in the evaluations of investors and traders. In isolation, these data permit only of tabulation; in association, they can perhaps be interpreted.

Of necessity, the rise in loans and investments was closely approximated by a rise in deposits. Between June, 1922, and December, 1929, total deposits increased about 17½ billion dollars, while loans and investments of all banks increased 18½ billion dollars. Loans rose, absolutely and relatively, more rapidly than investments, for they increased by 14 billion dollars or 50 per cent, while investments showed an advance of only 4 billion dollars or 33 per cent.[4]

These marked additions to deposits, based upon expanding assets, were legally dependent upon increases in the gold supply and in member bank reserve balances; indirectly, they reflected a desire of the public to secure credit and a willingness of the banking community to buy the proffered investments and to loan on the available collateral. A study of the behavior of money during the New Era must therefore largely concern itself with the changing composition of bank portfolios. The analysis of bank assets is, however, difficult; statistics, though available, are highly deceptive. A loan on securities may be used to purchase inventories, just as the funds made available by the sale of commercial paper may be utilized to purchase securities. If qualitative studies are not to be sacrificed, these several categories must, however, be accepted, at least as first approximations.

For many decades, loans on commercial paper were

considered crucially important; to facilitate the movement of goods from producer to consumer was, in fact, held to be the *raison d'être* of commercial banking. With the establishment of the Federal Reserve System, this theory was transformed into law, for rediscount privileges were specifically limited to "notes, drafts and bills of exchange issued or drawn for agricultural, industrial or commercial purposes or the proceeds of which have been used or are to be used for such purposes." Of interest in this connection is the fact that in 1914 loans based upon commercial paper represented less than half of all earning assets of National Banks. By the end of the postwar boom (1920), the ratio had risen to almost 60 per cent, but thereafter it declined rapidly. In 1929, commercial loans amounted to 37 per cent of the earning assets of National Banks. Selected studies reinforce the evidence about the decline in the commercial loan. In 1922, "all other loans"—a first approximation of commercial loans—of "reporting member banks" totaled a little more than 7 billion dollars, or 50 per cent of total loans and investments; in 1929, the absolute total had increased by 2 billion, but there had taken place a relative decline of almost 20 per cent. Between 1925 and 1930, "all other loans" of all "member banks" showed not only a relative but also an absolute decline. Further confirmation of this trend can be obtained from the fact that in 1923 about 30 per cent of all loans of National Banks were eligible for rediscount, while in 1929 only 20 per cent of the loan portfolio could qualify. Moreover, between 1924 and 1929 there was a shrinkage of 70 per cent in the volume of business in the commercial-paper market.[5]

These developments were viewed with concern. Toward the end of the twenties, the Federal Reserve Bank of New York sought to discover to what extent corporations were increasing their business while reducing their short-time indebtedness to the banks. A sample of 39 companies revealed that during five years (1922 to 1927) the ratio of capital funds to current debt increased 70 per cent while bank debt declined 20 per cent; unfortunately data relating to inventories were unobtainable. Only two out of six industries showed increased borrowings.[6]

A more detailed study of 700 corporations with total assets at the end of the New Era of 11 billion dollars showed an unmistakable trend. In 1922-23, inventories totaled approximately 4 billion dollars and notes payable (the proximate equivalent of bank loans) were 720 million dollars. By the end of the decade, investments in inventories had increased by one billion dollars, while notes payable shrank 300 million dollars or 40 per cent. The ratio of bank loans to inventories declined from 17 per cent in 1922 to 8.5 per cent in 1928. Only four of a total of thirty industries showed a rising ratio: department stores, paper, coal mining, and copper.[7]

The rise of deposits during the twenties was definitely not based upon increases in commercial loans, though the postwar boom that ended so disastrously in 1920 had been predicated on such an advance. Since many had serious, and not a few had insurmountable, difficulties in meeting their bank loans during the liquidation of 1920-21, the experience was not soon forgotten. Through-

101

out the twenties, corporations strove valiantly to remain free of indebtedness to the banks; in general, they were highly successful, for large earnings facilitated the accumulation of working capital, and the stock-market boom insured that short-term as well as long-term funds could be obtained from new flotations.[8]

If the rise in deposits during the twenties be correlated with changes in the loan portfolios of the banks, particular attention must be devoted to the important categories of real estate and securities. For many years, the law stood between National Banks and real-estate loans; the prohibitions were so stringent that in 1922 loans on "other real estate" (excluding farm land) totaled 160 million dollars, only 1.4 per cent of all loans. As the decade progressed, the banks took it upon themselves to change the status of mortgage paper, and the passage of the McFadden-Pepper bill in 1926 legalized these actions. Of particular importance was the provision extending the maturity period of nonfarm mortgage paper from one to five years. In 1929, these loans exceeded one billion dollars, an increase of almost 700 per cent in seven years.[9]

Mutual Savings Banks undertook the most rapid expansion in their holdings of urban real-estate paper, the total rising from 2,400 million dollars in 1921 to 5,200 million dollars in 1929. Loan and Trust Companies showed an even faster rate of increase—480 to 1,400 million dollars; the changes in State Banks and Stock Savings Banks were slight. If the experience of all banks during the twenties be summed up, it becomes clear that the increase of loans on real estate, from 5 to 10 billion dollars, was absolutely and relatively more marked than the rise in commercial loans.[10]

During this same period, developments in the farm-loan market were less impressive. Between 1922 and 1929 the twelve Federal Land Banks increased their loans upon mortgages from 600 to 1,200 million dollars and the Joint Stock Land Banks expanded their portfolios from 200 to 600 million dollars. National Banks increased their holdings of farm paper slightly: 200 to 300 million dollars. Although the twenties witnessed an increase of more than 100 per cent in bank loans on farm real estate, the absolute figures were considerably smaller than those for urban real estate: the former increased from 1,000 to 2,100 million dollars; the latter, from 5 to 10 billion dollars.[11]

At the beginning of the twenties, Veblen suggested that real estate rather than poker should be known as "The Great American Game"; at the end of the twenties he might well have nominated the stock market. In 1922, 26 per cent of the loans of all National Banks were secured by stocks and bonds, a figure that rose during the twenties until it reached 35 per cent in 1929. Although "all other city banks" and "country banks" participated in the advance, the most striking increase occurred in the holdings of "New York City banks." The absolute figures are even more impressive. In June, 1921, it is estimated that total loans of all banks on securities amounted to 7,600 million dollars; in October, 1929, they were in excess of 20 billion dollars. If the "reporting member banks" be singled out for study, corroborative evidence is obtained, for their security loans increased from 4 to 8 billion dollars between 1922 and 1929.[12]

The banks accommodated customers and brokers alike; in 1922, the former borrowed 2½ and the latter 1½ billion dollars. In 1929, the corresponding figures were roughly twice as large. During the intervening period, diverse tendencies were manifest. In 1922, 1924, 1925, and 1927 brokers' loans increased rapidly, while loans to customers remained stable or actually declined. The advance in brokers' loans during the twenties was indeed phenomenal, for in August, 1921, they totaled 750 million dollars and in the fall of 1929 they exceeded 9 billion dollars. When brokers' loans increased from approximately 6 to 9 billion dollars in the twelve months following October, 1928, almost the entire advance was financed by nonbanking groups: corporations, individuals, investment trusts, and foreign accounts. At the time of the crash, their funds in the call market totaled 6½ billion dollars.[13]

Superficially, the banks played a minor role during the final spurt of the security markets. Loans financed by funds from "the account of others" did not create additional deposits but rather energized old ones. Hence, increases in velocity helped considerably to support an increased volume of sales at enhanced prices. After the October crash, moreover, the nonbanking loans shrank with unbelievable rapidity; between October 4 and December 31, 4 out of a total of 6½ billion dollars were withdrawn. The "reporting member banks" followed suit by reducing their loans to brokers from 2,800 to 1,600 million dollars, or almost 45 per cent. In the midst of this liquidation, banks increased their loans to customers from 4,800 to 6,300 million dollars, a most unusual advance for a period that witnessed a shrinkage in the value of all securities listed on the New York Stock Exchange from 90 to 64 billion dollars. Yet, if the panic were not to be turned into a rout, it was necessary to fill the void created by the withdrawal of nonbanking funds.[14]

During the twenties while the total loan portfolio of the banks expanded rapidly, the most striking increases occurred in the sector devoted to real estate and securities. In addition, investments increased from 12 to 16 billion dollars, a rise that was not associated, however, with any marked changes in composition.

During the World War, National Banks increased their holdings of United States government bonds very rapidly; in 1916 they totaled only 30 per cent of all investments, while in 1919 they represented more than 60 per cent. Thereafter, they declined steadily. Between 1922 and 1929 United States government bonds as a percentage of total investments of National Banks declined one fifth. During these years, railroad bonds also lost position, the bonds of minor jurisdictions increased slightly, and public-service and miscellaneous bonds grew more rapidly. Bonds of foreign governments and corporations composed about 10 per cent of the total investment portfolio of National Banks.[15]

The increase of 17 billion dollars in the loans and investments of all banks between 1922 and 1929—13

billion dollars in loans and 4 billion dollars in investments
—was paralleled by an increase of approximately 16 billion dollars in deposits—11 billion dollars in time and 5
billion dollars in demand deposits. Since many students
contend that only demand deposits can affect the structure of prices and production, it is important to study
bank liabilities before evaluating the changes in bank
assets.

As early as 1909, time deposits equaled 25 per cent
of the total deposits of commercial banks (including
National Banks and Loan and Trust Companies). In
volume, they totaled approximately 2½ billion dollars.
The Federal Reserve Act prescribed a lower reserve requirement for time than for demand deposits; thereafter
the former increased rapidly, both absolutely and relatively. In 1922, time deposits amounted to 17½ billion
dollars or just less than 50 per cent of all deposits. By
the end of the New Era they had increased 11 billion
dollars and represented 56 per cent of all deposits.[16]

Because bona-fide savings accounts have a negligible
velocity, most students have failed to count them as effective money. Of late, evidence, direct and indirect, has
been accumulating which throws considerable doubt upon
the placidity of many time deposits. For instance, during
the New Era they grew most rapidly in cities over 100,-
000; a sizable proportion were in accounts of more than
25 thousand dollars; in metropolitan areas their velocity
was considerable; fluctuations in time deposits of member
banks were markedly greater than fluctuations in the
deposits of Mutual Savings Banks. If the effectiveness of

money be described in terms of its velocity, then many time deposits were money just as many demand deposits were not.[17]

A markedly lower reserve requirement for time than for demand deposits facilitated an accelerated rise in total deposits. Since many time deposits were not inactive, and since the prevalence of time deposits stimulated the banks to purchase investments with high yields, only a taxonomist would deny that time deposits were money.[18]

Since the creation of new deposits and the survival of old deposits depend upon the quantity and quality of banking assets, the behavior of money during the New Era can be appreciated only if the portfolios of the banks are critically evaluated. For the greater part of a century, orthodox theory believed that it was the duty of commercial banks to finance goods in process from producer to consumer but not to finance either producer or consumer. The severe liquidation of 1920-21 proved that under the stimulus of inventory speculation, commercial loans could rise rapidly and conceal for a considerable period the dangers of such a rise. During the twenties, increases in bank deposits were a reflection, in the first instance, of increases in loans on real estate and securities and, in the second, of increases in investments. Convinced that these assets could be liquidated only with difficulty, conservatives viewed the trend with alarm. Nor were their fears put to rest by the contentions of the optimists who pointed out that nothing was more liquid than loans on securities, because securities could be sold within an hour's notice. Skeptics added to the confusion by emphasizing that a banking system, in contradistinction to a single bank, could never be liquid and any attempt to achieve such a condition could only lead to universal insolvency.

The liquidity of a bank depends upon the vendibility of its assets, which in turn depends largely upon the public's evaluation of the future. Implicit in the commercial theory of banking is the short duration of the average loan, for a strong presumption exists in favor of correct analyses of the near rather than the more distant future. If only a few weeks or months need pass between the granting of a loan and its repayment, mistakes can be kept within bounds. It is improbable that the price level and the volume of business will fluctuate so greatly within a few months as to endanger more than a small percentage of commercial loans. The collapse of 1920 was the exception. Moreover, commercial loans are usually granted upon commodities in national and international trade, so that, in addition to the frequency of testing, the criteria of testing are more reliable. Local abnormalities are reduced to a minimum.

The growing importance of investment assets as a percentage of all earning assets—in the case of National Banks the rise during the twenties was almost 50 per cent —can now be more easily appreciated. Although securities and houses may be bought today for sale tomorrow, substantial activity in the security and real-estate markets is based upon the community's evaluation of the future trend of business earnings and the demand for housing. Years, rather than weeks or months, are involved in these estimates; and as the time lengthens, error becomes more probable. Within wide limits, incorrect estimates can, however, justify themselves.[19]

Traders are in constant association with other traders and their evaluations of the future are in largest measure group responses. This mutuality of stimulation subjects many markets to cumulative tendencies, especially those markets in which prices depend upon estimates of the far-distant future. Within considerable periods of time, the expectations of the mass, despite their certain inaccuracy, alone determine the prices of securities and real estate. Until the facts become crystal clear, errors can accumulate and remain hidden. Herein lay the crucial danger in the altered composition of bank portfolios during the twenties.[20]

As traders became increasingly optimistic about the future value of stocks and real estate, they sought accommodation from the banks in order to enlarge their sphere of operations. The willingness of the banks to extend loans secured by these assets implied that virgin deposits depended for their existence upon the maintenance of these newly established values. Of course, the creation of new money by the banking system helped to justify these optimistic expectations of the future, for it acted as a stimulant to prices and production.

Although building and loan associations and life-insurance companies played the major roles in the expansion of the urban real-estate market during the twenties, the increase of 5 billion dollars in bank loans secured by real estate must have contributed greatly to intensifying the expansion. Between 1921 and 1929, the urban real-estate mortgage debt jumped from 9 to more than 27 billion dollars, a phenomenal advance for such a short period. In fact, if complete data were obtainable, the figure at the end of the New Era might approximate 35 billion dollars.[21]

The New Era will always be remembered for the behavior of the stock market, which was probably without parallel in the history of this or any other country. There is good reason to believe that the marked increase in bank loans upon securities—in June, 1921, they totaled less than 8 billion dollars, while in October, 1929, they stood in the neighborhood of 20 billion—must have accelerated trading on the exchange. After the middle of the decade, new records were being constantly established. In 1925, the number of shares traded exceeded 300 million, breaking the record of 1919; in 1928, the figure had tripled, and by the following year the billion mark had been passed. Between 1922 and 1929, the price of a seat on the exchange rose from 100 to 600 thousand dollars. New offerings mounted rapidly; in 1926, 79 issues composed of 57 million shares were placed on the market; in 1929, the corresponding figures were 173 issues and 188 million shares. Most impressive was the increase in the value of securities, which rose from 27 billion dollars in 1925 to 90 billion dollars at the end of the New Era, an advance of more than 300 per cent in less than five years.[22]

The rise in equities was in large measure based upon the marked increases in the activity of the economy, with its concomitant large returns on old investments and its promise of still larger returns on new investments. Between 1922 and 1929, the national income rose from 60 to more than 80 billion dollars. This represented a per capita gain of approximately 25 per cent, a truly remarkable advance. During these years, property income payments rose steadily from 6,600 million dollars in 1922 to 11,300 million dollars in 1929; the cumulative total was about 70 billion dollars. Despite the higher level of consumption that is usually associated with a period of increasing production and profits, the returns to the owners of property were so enlarged that a presumption exists in favor of a rapid rise in the savings of individuals. During this period, the net savings of business enterprises likewise mounted rapidly; for the seven years, they aggregated 20 billion dollars.[23]

Since unemployed money is not eligible for relief, it has generally been put to work. Only substantial fears about the future can keep it idle. During the twenties, the prevailing optimism ensured that the larger portion of the savings of individuals and corporations would be invested. Between 1922 and 1929, net new capital issues floated in the United States for domestic and foreign borrowing totaled approximately 50 billion dollars; the average annual rate of change was in excess of 8 per cent. In addition, corporations plowed back about 20 billion dollars. Unfortunately, so little is known of the nature and composition of the savings of individuals that it is impossible to break down the sources of the funds for capital formation. Data relating to national income suggest, however, that the rise in aggregate production was so rapid during the New Era as to facilitate increases in savings, corporate and individual.[24]

But the story continues. The twenties witnessed an expansion of approximately 16 billion dollars in bank deposits, in large measure the reflection of increased loans on securities and real estate. Changing ciphers on the books of the banks doubtless stimulated the production of goods and services, but it likewise contributed to advancing the prices of equities. The expansion of the economy, to which the banks contributed materially by increasing the money supply, generated a highly optimistic evaluation of future prospects. In harmony with these rosy expectations, bank assets were revalued upward. If the estimates were revised, assets could not fail to shrink. In the fall of 1929, the estimates were radically revised. The value of all securities on the New York Stock Exchange declined about 30 billion dollars within three months; real estate reacted in sympathy. Confronted with a radical shrinkage in the equities underlying their loans, the banks sought desperately to safeguard their depositors. Fearful of the future, they called old loans and refused to grant new ones. With the passage of every month, the liquidation of bank deposits became more intense.

The review of the banking mechanism during the New Era discloses several interesting facts: that a comparatively small rise of 700 million dollars in member bank balances permitted an increase of 13 billion dollars in loans and 4 billion dollars in investments, which in turn

112

was correlated with an addition of 16 billion dollars in the money supply. Further, that the lending policies of banks were, of necessity, greatly influenced by bankers' expectations of the future. Finally, that the structure of prices and production was influenced as much by money created by the banks as by savings garnered from industry and trade. The dynamics of the New Era are to be sought in these interrelations.

CHAPTER VI

THE NEW ERA

THE New Era, like every era, will always defy comprehensive analysis, for the strategic factors of economics are too many and too variable to permit of more than impressionistic treatment. The retreat from the facts does not imply, however, that all retreats are equally valid. If theory be not contradicted by the facts, it is probable that the essentials have been comprehended, the unessentials disregarded. Unless theory be subjected to this test, its validity can be gauged only by inner consistency, only by the rules of logic. But experience alone permits the logic of the sane to be differentiated from that of the insane.

Economic data always serve two purposes: they facilitate the measuring of change between the present and the more immediate past, and they likewise establish a base for forecasting the more immediate future. For instance, the course of wages during the twenties proved that labor enjoyed a standard of living substantially superior to that of former years; the same materials also facilitated the growth of the high-wage doctrine of prosperity. The marked stability in wholesale prices, with the concomitant slow decline in the price of manufactured goods and the slow rise in the price of agricultural products, shed considerable light upon the changing structure of income and costs. Moreover, the data served as a foundation for correlating the basic stability of prices with the basic stability of the economy. Evidence relating to the rapid rise in aggregate profits proved that the major sectors of industry were securing satisfactory returns upon their investments; the failure of profit ratios to rise convinced most observers that the increased earnings were a function of enhanced efficiency, not of financial manipulations. In general, the signposts of the twenties permitted of one conclusion: that the advance of the economy which had resulted in the highest per capita production in the history of the country could long continue. The foundation was strong.

During the twenties, the rapid accumulation of factual materials and the rising prestige of detailed analyses were mutually stimulating, with the result that few students ventured attempts at general synthesis. The herculean task of assimilating the welter of data encouraged preoccupation with specific problems. Forced to estimate future trends, the business community could not, however, avoid general deductions. Each of the major signposts supported an inclusive theory of economic development—wages, the high-wage doctrine; prices, the stable-price doctrine; profits, the constancy of profit ratios. So strong was the optimistic tradition that the congruity of the several criteria was not analyzed. The collapse of the New Era in the fall of 1929 proved that, although the economic system was radically transformed during the twenties, the processes of transformation remained hidden, even from the view of experts. A complete explanation is still impossible, but a first approach may be ventured.

The operations of a modern economy may be viewed from three angles: the production of goods and services (technological); evaluations of the future prospects of business (psychological); exchange of goods, services, and capital (monetary). Of course, this framework could be vastly complicated but simplification, that stops short of false abstraction, is valuable. It can perhaps be utilized in dissociating the prosperity of the twenties from the illusion of its stability.

Although changes in the psychology of the business community or in the volume of bank deposits may materially affect the operations of an economy, the most important factor in modern economic life remains the technological. Industrial capitalism has been transformed by houses in construction, wheat in harvest, trains in transit. The marriage between physical science and profit enterprise has long been fertile, though occasionally it has been subject to abortion.

During the World War, when governmental agencies undertook the work formerly performed by private exchanges, severe limitations were placed upon the untrammeled progress of technology. To insure the defeat of the foe, policies were adopted that resulted in stimulating the metals and depressing the nonmetallics; agricultural acreage and livestock holdings increased, while the production of nonessentials declined.

European purchases of our goods with our money delayed for several years the readjustment of the war to a peace economy. Exports before the outbreak of the World War had averaged 2 billion dollars annually while in each of the three years 1918, 1919, 1920 they totaled 7 billion. In 1920, the postponement was at an end: prices dropped precipitously, commercial failures multiplied, the number of unemployed jumped by millions. By midsummer of 1921, the liquidation had more or less spent itself; within the next six months, business improved noticeably. Despite large crops, farm prices increased, enlarging farm incomes. Building activity, seriously curtailed during the war and immediate postwar years, recovered once prices were partially readjusted; in 1921, urban construction broke all records; additions to, and redistribution of, population during the preceding years facilitated the emergence of profit margins. The rolling-stock of the railroads had deteriorated during the interlude of governmental control; hence, as soon as the intense liquidation had exhausted itself, orders were placed for new equipment. The automobile industry, the fastest-growing large industry in the country—in 1913-14 its annual output totaled 500 thousand vehicles, while in 1919-20 production was four times as great—had slumped badly after midsummer of 1920 but managed to recover within twelve months. In 1922, total production exceeded 2½ million cars, or 22 per cent in excess of the former record of 1920. Only a radical shrinkage in total national income such as occurred in 1920-21 could have depressed the automobile industry; improvements in production, paralleled by improvements in distribution, ensured that the industry would continue for some time to enjoy a sellers' market. The combined advances of the construction, automobile, and railroad-equipment industries stimulated production and employment directly and indirectly; they were in largest measure responsible for the recovery of the iron and steel industry during the first half of 1922. The emergence of the country from its most rapid liquidation though by no means its most severe depression has barely been outlined by these few facts and figures. But our interest lies in the years that follow. In one respect, the early and the later twenties are intimately associated: it appears that the two industries—automobiles and construction—that played a strategic role in shortening the period of readjustment after the liquidation of 1920-21 were also responsible for prolonging the expansion once it got under way.[1]

Outstanding in the industrial development of the twenties was the expansion of the automobile industry. At the beginning of the decade, total registration figures were approximately 9 million; by the end of the New Era they had increased threefold. Annual production averaged about 2 million units in 1920-23, while in 1927-29 it totaled more than 4½ million. The dollar value of new cars, parts, and accessories mounted rapidly, though at a slightly slower rate than the physical volume of production; in 1922, output of the industry at wholesale was 2½ billion dollars and in 1929 it exceeded 5 billion dollars.[2]

So rapid an expansion led to marked increases in the number of employees and the size of the payroll, as well as to enlarged investments in plant and machinery. Moreover, the important complementary industries of gasoline and rubber tires were greatly stimulated; in 1929, 84 per cent of crude rubber and 80 per cent of domestic gasoline were consumed by motor vehicles. Finally, a sizable proportion of the total output of steel, copper, lumber, cotton, and many minor industries was absorbed in the production of automobiles.[3]

The rapid penetration of the automobile into American economic life was largely responsible for the expansion of suburbs, the relocation of minor industries, the rise of vacation resorts. Distribution patterns were altered; the mail-order houses found it necessary to enter direct retailing. Of course, the highway system was vastly extended and improved; in 1929, total expenditures for road building and upkeep totaled 2 billion dollars. Metaphors used by politicians best illustrate the change: chickens in the pot made way for cars in the garage. In fact, many unaccustomed to fowl were well acquainted with "Lizzies."[4]

Intimately related to the expansion of automobile production was the rapid rise in construction. It has already been emphasized that during the immediate postwar years building activity slackened radically: for each of the four years after 1917, new construction was approximately one third less than it had been during the four years preceding our entrance into the war. The physical volume of new building reached a low in 1920 when it amounted to less than half of the 1913 total. Thereafter, conditions changed radically and rapidly: 1921 showed almost

119

100 per cent improvement over 1920; 1922, another 50 per cent improvement over 1921. During the early twenties, the expansion was most marked in residential and nonhousekeeping dwellings (hotels, clubs, lodging houses); in 1921 the total value of all residential construction totaled 1,800 million dollars, while in 1925 it exceeded 4,700 million dollars. Commercial building spurted in the middle and again at the end of the decade; utilities, public works, and institutional building evidenced a more even rate of growth. The total value of new construction amounted to more than 4 billion dollars in 1922; and at the end of the New Era it exceeded 7 billion dollars, an increase of 70 per cent.[5]

The expansion of the construction industry, like the expansion of automobile industry, must not be judged solely in terms of its own product. The welfare of such important industries as steel, lumber, cement, electrical supplies depended in large part upon construction. Building materials, in crude and finished form, represented one eighth of all freight tonnage. Though local conditions resulted in construction reaching its peak in Southern California in 1923, in Florida and Philadelphia in 1925, in New York in 1926, the 50 billion dollars of new construction erected between 1922 and 1929 certainly helped "to stabilize and act as a tonic on general business conditions."[6]

If the 3½ billion dollar annual contribution of the automobile industry and the 7 billion dollar product of the construction industry loomed most important during the New Era, other sectors of the economy helped the expansion along. Industrial capitalism has always witnessed the emergence of new industries; the twenties were no exception. Most important was the phenomenal growth of the radio industry, whose total sales mounted from 2 million dollars in 1920 to 850 million dollars in 1929. Direct employment was furnished to one hundred thousand workers and, if broadcasting, selling, and servicing activities be included, the figures would show an even more rapid rise.[7]

On a smaller scale, the twenties witnessed accelerated developments in other industries. Between 1921 and 1929, the value of aircraft production increased approximately a thousandfold. Practically unknown at the beginning of the decade, the rayon industry had an annual output of 150 million dollars at the end of the New Era. The product of the motion-picture industry increased in value 250 per cent in eight years. Of the older and well-established industries, electrical manufacturing made substantial advances, for its total production increased during the decade from 800 to 2,300 million dollars; the sales of mechanical refrigerators alone amounted to 160 million dollars in 1929.[8]

Free from the plague of excess capacity, "new industries" derive strategic importance from the fact that increases in the demand for their products necessitate considerable expansion in the manufacture of productive equipment. Frequently, this stimulation spreads to complementary industries; the rapid increase in the demand for automobiles during the early twenties forced Detroit to add to its capacity and it also led many suppliers of automobile parts and materials to enlarge their plants.

Moreover, highways had to be improved and filling stations multiplied. The age of an industry greatly influences the degree of primary and secondary stimulation that follows upon enlarged demands for its products. An increase of two million units in the manufacture of motor vehicles such as occurred in the early twenties had repercussions considerably more intense than did a similar increase between 1933 and 1935.[9]

Typical of depressions are reduced expenditures for maintenance, replacements, and inventories. Although the liquidation of 1920-21 was colored by the World War, there is little reason to doubt that, once total spendings began to increase, a tendency followed for an intensified expansion in the production of capital goods. The noticeable spurt in the production of automobiles and railroad equipment that marked the beginnings of the recovery can in part be explained in terms of delayed replacements and the need for additional capacity. Moreover, the activity of the building industry, which contributed so greatly to the expansion of the New Era, can likewise be illumined by the technical relation between consumer expenditures and their intensified reflection on the production of capital goods. The ability to increase one's rent by 50 dollars per month and a belief in the continuance of this enlarged outlay may well lead to 6,000 dollars of new construction.[10]

Although the modern businessman makes decisions on the basis of prices and costs in much the same manner that the medieval mystic regulated his life by the Cabala, he can never emancipate himself from technological forces whose influence remains all-powerful. The expansion of new industries and the stimulation of old industries formed the foundation for the New Era. Activity in one sector was diffused to other sectors; in turn, the process was reversed. Enlarged demand for consumers' goods led to increased production of capital equipment; but the purchase of labor and materials by the latter insured an enlarged demand for the former. Once the spiral of increased productive activity, increased income, larger productive activity, still larger incomes was set off in 1921-22, the support afforded by the automobile and construction industries, later aided by the radio, electrical, and other industries, formed the foundation for seven years of a markedly sustained expansion.[11]

For a century and more, economists attempted to explain normal behavior in terms of rationality. The felicific calculus of Bentham and the dialectical materialism of Marx are more closely associated than the followers of either would care to admit. Both are mechanistic; both ascribe a transcendental importance to pecuniary evaluations. The eighteenth century was wiser, for it knew that rationality was an ideal, not an actuality; the twentieth century is slowly rediscovering this truth. First Veblen, then Pigou, more recently Keynes, in their analyses of business fluctuations, have ascribed a position of priority to the cumulation of errors in future estimates. Economic data reflect past activity and the interpretations of economic data condition future activity. Business enterprise is channeled between the realities of the past and the expectations of the future.[12]

The prevalence of unused capacity usually ensures, especially if raw materials and labor costs do not rise, that small increases in the gross volume of business will be accompanied by large increases in net profits. A heightening of productive activity, such as occurred toward the end of 1921, was associated with a rise in earnings; in addition, capital values were altered, for the latter are determined "by the current rate of interest, weighted by consideration of any prospective change in earning capacity." The optimism engendered by the expansion of the automobile and construction industries was soon diffused; advances in one sector bespeak advances in others.[13]

If new investment was the key to the expansion of the twenties, the capitalization process was its lock. The rise in the value of equities facilitated increases in bank loans and the money supply, so that the funds for new investment did not depend upon a curtailment of current consumption. It was a charmed circle: industrial expansion, enlarged earnings, increases in capitalization, facilitation of new investment, more expansion, larger earnings, further increases in the value of equities.

An increase in the total net income of all corporations from 4,700 million dollars in 1922 to 8,700 million dollars in 1929—an advance as large as it was steady—was assuredly a sound basis for the upward reevaluation of shares. Nor could there have been much doubt that as the swamps of yesterday were turned into the resorts of tomorrow real estate would rise in value. As rich Northerners began to winter in Florida and retired Iowans began to rejuvenate under the California sun, marked increases in the demand for land could not fail to be reflected in a rise in prices.

During the twenties, common stocks and mortgage bonds were the foci of the capitalization movement; inevitable, for industry and real estate accounted for an overwhelming portion of the country's total wealth. For decades, the stock market had offered the best method of adjusting the prices of liquid claims to the earning power of industrial assets. True, if the records of old were dusted, a determinate relation was not easily discernible; but if extremes were eliminated, ten times annual earnings had long been considered an appropriate price. Sample studies revealed that in 1922 the ratio of prices to earnings for a representative list was: motor, 7; merchandising, 7; oils, 9; steel, 9; electrical equipment, 10; railroads, 13; chemicals, 15. By 1927, the ratios had mounted moderately, though the advances in merchandising and equipment shares had been rapid. At the height of the boom, the ratio for motors was only 10 and for steel 15, but oils were selling at 29 times earnings, electrical equipment at 30, and merchandising at 50![14]

The rapid rise in the ratios during the New Era was doubtless a reflection of a widespread belief not only in the permanence of the prosperity but also in its intensification. Enhanced industrial activity would lead to higher earnings, which in turn would reduce the ratios. Further, as capitalistic economies grew older there was good reason to believe that the customary rate of return on capital would tend to fall. The ease with which corporations were able to finance their own expansions, and the superfluity of funds in the capital markets, pointed to a fall in the interest rate, coincidental with marked increases in the supply of loanable funds.[15]

Although these factors might explain the moderate rise in the ratios for steel and motors during the twenties, they could not account for the striking increase in the ratios for electrical equipment and merchandising shares. Despite the large profits of industry toward the end of the New Era, returns on high-grade bonds frequently exceeded those on common stocks. Here was *a priori* evidence that the price level of securities was untenable.

The stock market was not solely concerned with the pricing of old investments and the facilitation of new flotations; clearly, it catered to the gambling proclivities of the American public. The phenomenal rise in the ratios of selling prices to earnings could only have reflected a demand founded on speculation rather than investment.[16]

Toward the end of the twenties, speculation in stocks was maintained by the shrewdness of veterans and the enthusiasm of recruits. Yet every sale brought the day of reckoning closer. The increasing disproportion between the return on stocks and that on other investments could not remain hidden; upon recognition, liquidation was in order. The structure of the body economic foreordained that cumulative tendencies so prominent during the advance would also be present in retreat.[17]

The change in the capitalization process during the New Era was founded on profits, though supported by speculation. Early in the twenties, increases in aggregate profits were a function of the widening gap between total receipts and total costs, a first consequence of an enlarged demand. Optimism engendered by these increased profits could have been justified only on the assumption that alterations in the conditions of supply and demand during the ensuing period would not depress the rate of return. Scarcity of the factors of production, however, made it improbable that marked increases in productive activity could continue without stimulating a rise in costs. More important, there was reason to fear that once the basic demand for automobiles and modernized housing was satisfied among the wealthy and well-to-do classes, it would prove difficult, if not impossible, to exploit the latent demand of the poor. Finally, intense competition might well lead to faulty investments. Large profits awaited the builders of the tallest edifice in the world, but height could not be patented. Excess capacity, the scourge of many industries during the New Era, was in part a reflection of activity engendered by prospective profits. Since these profits were frequently capitalized, their failure to materialize would necessitate a revision in the price of equities.[18]

Between 1925 and 1929 the aggregate value of all shares on the New York Stock Exchange increased from 27 to almost 100 billion dollars. Though this rise could be explained in terms of the increasing profits of industry and a widespread conviction of further increases in these profits, overwhelming evidence points to the strategic role of speculation, especially during the last period of the boom. During the twenties, the total volume of new private construction approximated 40 billion dollars. These years also witnessed an expansion in total urban mortgage debt from

9 to 27 billion dollars. A representative sample of a selected number of cities shows an increase in the assessed valuation of urban real estate from 42 to 67 billion dollars. Part of the rise in realty values can doubtless be explained in terms of real changes in market demand and investment, but part must probably be explained in terms of the capitalization of prospective earnings. Speculation did not play favorites.[19]

Since a one per cent increase in the rate of return frequently leads to a 20 per cent rise in the price of the asset, moderate changes in profitability presage considerable fluctuations in capitalization. Moreover, the importance of futurity implies that the demarcation between investment and speculation must always be indistinct.

In large part, the expansion of the economy during the New Era led to changes in capitalization but these changes in turn influenced the economy. The banking system was the go-between. Between 1922 and 1929, 16 billion dollars were added to our money supply; demand deposits increased 5 billion dollars and time deposits jumped more than 11 billion dollars. Parallel thereto, were increases of 17 billion dollars in bank loans and investments based largely on real estate and securities.[20]

During the depression of 1920-21, bank deposits declined in excess of 2 billion dollars; but as business advanced after midsummer of 1921, they commenced to rise rapidly. In the ensuing three years, they showed a gain of 8 billion dollars; the rates of increase in demand and time deposits were about equal. Substantial accretions to our gold supply afforded the banking system an opportunity to expand, and the enhanced demand of the business community for credit ensured that the opportunity would not be missed. Potential profitability helped stem the depression, while realized profits supported the expansion. Though manufacturing corporations earned only 3 billion dollars in 1921, their net returns for 1922 were almost 8 billion dollars and in the following year they totaled nine and a half billion dollars. These enlarged profits led to a revised capitalization of equities, above all to increases in the prices of real estate and securities. The enhancement in the value of collateral enabled the banking system to enlarge its loans and thus to add directly to the supply of money.[21]

The processes of saving and investment hold the key to business expansion and contraction, yet no key is more difficult to find. Typically, saving is not accomplished by the accumulation of a stock of consumable goods possessed of the power to protect the individual directly from hunger, cold, or boredom. In the last analysis, additions to and improvements in the physical plant of the country can result only from the more efficient and more intense utilization of available material and human resources. True, it has long been contended by economic theorists that increases in the production of capital equipment necessitate a transference of purchasing power from the satiated to the enterprising. A venerable theory, but one of questionable validity. There is little ground to believe that increases in the production of capital equipment will be stimulated if increased savings are deflected from the purchase of products capable of manufacture by the new equipment. The total volume of output can probably be increased by additions to, but not by reallocation of, available resources. Depressions indicate the prevalence of unemployed men and empty factories; recovery depends upon the mating of the two without simultaneously encouraging new divorces. Investment must await entrepreneurial expectations that the existing level of consumption will not shrink; better still, that it may expand. In the short run, profits depend much more upon increases in the volume than upon improvements in the efficiency of production. Here the banks enter. Possessed of the ability to enlarge their loans and investments and thereby increase the supply of money, they can facilitate the merger of unemployed men and unused resources without placing any strain upon income available for consumption. The twenties are a case in point.[22]

In 1920-21, millions of men were without work, thousands of machines without tenders. Increased activity depended upon new investment, which in turn was contingent upon the supply and utilization of available funds. Savings are in large part a function of income, and a depression is typified by marked contractions in income. During the first twelve months of the postwar collapse, the national income declined approximately 14 billion dollars or 20 per cent. Because of the radical reduction in prices, the decline in money income exaggerates the decline in the production of goods and services. However, if funds for new investment had depended solely upon savings from past or current income, they might have been insufficient to support a marked expansion. The creation of new money by the banks assured entrepreneurs that their new investments would not precipitate a reduction in consumption; further, it helped to keep the price of new capital within bounds. Alone, the banks could not have forced the expansion; but working in a favorable environment of marked shortages in construction, vast improvements in the manufacture and sale of automobiles, a high level of wages, delayed modernization of plants, the banks were able to heighten prospective profits.[23]

Nor must it be assumed that the contribution of the banks to the prosperity of the twenties ceased after the first years of the decade. Large increases in the annual income, which rose from 60 to almost 85 billion dollars during the New Era, ensured that current savings would supply a large part of the funds necessary for expansion; the more so if it be true that increases in the income of the rich lead to accelerated increases in their savings. Yet this is not the entire story. Although demand and time deposits increased 8 billion dollars between 1921 and 1924, they increased an equal amount during the following four years. To neglect this advance would be as false as to overemphasize its importance.[24]

The congruence of forces, technological, psychological, and monetary, was responsible for the intense economic activity of the twenties. Money probably contributed to the birth and delayed the death of the New Era. By 1927, the economy gave evidence of severe strains; for the first time in several years, construction failed to advance and the automobile industry suffered a noticeable setback. The price of equities invited revision, for the retardation in the rate of growth of important industries foreshadowed a decline in their profits. To hold a national election under the auspices of declining trends was a prospect to be avoided at all costs, and the authorities in Washington strove valiantly to forestall the decline. The alleviation of all monetary stringency, which proved a boon to the British who were then engaged in revaluing the pound, considerably lightened the task of American speculators. Nor can there be much doubt that during the last two years of the New Era the rapid advance in the price of stocks contributed greatly to stimulating the economy at large. Founded on the expansion of the construction and automobile industries, inflamed by the optimism engendered by a period of rapid growth, the New Era from beginning to end was the beneficiary of an intoxicating monetary flow.[25]

To dissociate the reality of economic expansion during the twenties from the illusion of its permanence is no longer impossible. The pieces form a pattern. The striking improvement in the real annual income of labor during the decade was a fact beyond dispute. Moreover, it was correct to conclude, as did so many contemporary observers, that the welfare of many industries depended upon the purchasing power of the mass. Doubtful was only the doctrine of high wages that sought to explain the dynamics of the era by virtues inherent in raising wage rates. The data were sparse, and the logic was weak. With the exception of a few highly organized sectors of the labor market, wage rates failed to advance appreciably during the New Era. Despite popular misconceptions, employers found it impossible to pay more than the prevailing rate on the assumption that the rise in wage costs would more than be offset by returns from an enlarged volume of sales.

The failure of profit ratios to mount during the era was also viewed with great satisfaction, for stability in the return to capital was interpreted as absence of pathological conditions in the distribution of income. Of course, reformers did not cease believing that the rich were too rich and the poor too poor, but little fear was expressed that this differential would impede the general advance of the economy. Although the rate of industrial profits fluctuated within the narrow range of 9 to 12 per cent on capitalization, the net income of all corporations increased from 4,700 million dollars in 1922 to 8,700 million dollars in 1929.[26]

In isolation, the wage and profit signposts permitted of optimistic interpretations; in combination, they might well have raised questions about the future stability of the economy. Between 1922 and 1929, aggregate wages and salaries increased from 40 to 55 billion dollars while property income payments rose from 6,600 to 11,300 million dollars; the national income mounted from approximately 60 to 85 billion dollars. Since returns to labor and capital comprised the overwhelming proportion of the total, increased shares to each were clearly impossible; but not increased sums, for an expansion in total production could enrich both sectors simultaneously. It must not, however, be overlooked that the expansion was accompanied by marked additions to the supply and striking increases in the velocity of money. If logic suggested that the multiplication of goods and services was thereby facilitated, and if experience suggested that the flood might be followed by a drought, there were ample grounds for pessimism, if not despondency.[27]

Of all the signposts, none was more encouraging than the behavior of prices.* Unlike previous periods of economic expansion, the New Era was unique in that the level of wholesale prices failed to advance or decline, evincing a stability that led many to believe that the prosperity of no group was predicated upon the exploitation of another. Since judgment is almost exclusively determined by experience, and history is vicarious experience, the sanguineness can easily be appreciated. But the twenties witnessed an expansion in the physical volume of production of 4 per cent per annum; the total output of goods in 1929 was one third again as large as it had been in 1922. *A priori*, a decline in the price level was to be expected; its stability should therefore have been suspect. The more so when one recalls that the optimism of the era was greatly heightened by the decline in unit costs. If prices were stable and costs were declining, what of the differential; how did it emerge and what were its implications?

Contradictions in the signposts were frequently overlooked; pessimists were conspicuously absent. In part, the explanation can be sought in the neglect of tracing the

* Contemporaries placed great stress upon these signposts; witness the Report of the Committee on Recent Economic Changes:

"Thus the unit cost of production has been reduced." "Profits made from fluctuations . . . have tended to diminish." "A high wage level and a stationary cost of living created a phenomenon, now in degree. . . ." "The increasing tendency toward price stability . . ."

interrelations of banking and business; the behavior of money was primarily responsible for permitting the incompatible to live at peace. True, as the New Era approached its end, an increasing number of observers reflected upon the invidious connections between the banking system and the stock market, but, at worst, they feared a temporary and localized readjustment of stock prices. In part, failure to understand the dynamics of expansion must be explained in terms of the multiplicity of data and the inadequacy of theoretical tools. It is of interest that one of the few analysts who throughout the twenties clearly delineated the unstable factors failed to trust his own insight after history had proved him right. In November, 1929, he wrote that the economy was basically sound: inventories were not excessive; business was free from serious indebtedness to the banks; even stock prices were at reasonable levels—in short, a business crisis was absolutely precluded.[28]

The misinterpretation of future trends must in large part be ascribed to the persuasiveness of large numbers and to the basically optimistic hue of American business. Thought is always socially conditioned and deviations from the norm are always difficult and frequently dangerous. Moreover, competition is highly coercive. Survival in the long run depends in the first instance upon the protection of one's position in the short run. Imitation of a competitor's moves may clearly lead to future trouble; yet, failure to keep the pace implies certain death. Caught in a subtle conspiracy of forces both psychological and economic, the business community was unable to differen-

tiate during the New Era between the unstable foundation and the substantial façade.

To discern the untrustworthiness of the signposts of
stability was no easy matter, but the transience of the
economic expansion and its inevitable cessation could
have been deduced from evidence other than the signposts.
It was clear that the construction and automobile industries were of strategic importance in establishing and
maintaining the high level of economic activity typical of
the twenties. Directly and indirectly, they led to the investment of billions of dollars and to the employment of
millions of men. Hence, unless the rate of growth of these
key industries could have been maintained, or unless new
industries could have been developed, economic activity
was certain to slacken. The distribution of income in the
United States was a valuable clue to the future. It might
have been good politics but it was assuredly bad economics to talk of two cars in every garage when at the
high point of the prosperity 80 per cent of the families
in the country had a total income of 3,000 dollars or less,
and 97 per cent of all families were below the 10,000 dollar
bracket. Nor was there any probability that prices could
be lowered sufficiently to tap the latent demand of the
poor.[29]

The twenties were replete with evidence that the growth
curve for automobile production was leveling off: between
1921 and 1925, registration figures almost doubled; during the next four years, they increased but 25 per cent.
Much the same was true of housing. From 1920 to 1925,
the value of new residential construction mounted from

one to almost five billion dollars annually. Thereafter a slow but steady decline set in; in 1929, the total was approximately 50 per cent below 1925. Between 1922 and 1929, more than 6 million new dwelling units were constructed, a rate of expansion which indicated that the wealthy and middle classes were being amply supplied with adequate housing. Only by catering to the poor could this high level of building activity have been maintained; but unfortunately, private entrepreneurs had never been tempted to build for the poor. Toward the end of the New Era the prospects were hopeless, for money on the call market was able to earn between 6 and 12 per cent, the building trades were strongly organized, the construction-goods industries were disinclined to experiment with a flexible-price policy, and urban land values had been the object of speculative advances.[30]

After a most careful study of production trends in the United States since 1870, the best-informed student of the problem opines that "it is difficult to escape the conclusion that retardation in the growth of production has been almost universal among the industries covered, and that the rapidity of the retardation has been, on the whole, quite appreciable." If the serious repercussions in the slowing down of the construction and automobile industries were to have been avoided, the economy would have had to develop new industries of considerable magnitude. In 1928, the value of new construction totaled 7 billion dollars and the wholesale value of new motor vehicles exceeded 3 billion dollars. Radio, the fastest-growing large industry, had a total output of 650 million dollars in

1928 and of 850 million dollars in 1929, and even radio was already suffering from a marked retardation in its rate of growth. The magnitude of the automobile and construction industries made it highly improbable that any substantial slack in their production could be easily offset. The emergence of important industries is never accomplished overnight; only miniature golf courses come and go.[31]

Clearly, declines in important sectors of the economy could not be isolated. As the number of new dwellings and automobiles failed to increase from one year to another, or worse still if they suffered absolute declines, it was inevitable that associated industries would suffer grievously. Enlargement of means of production varies not with the volume of the demand for the finished product but rather with the acceleration of the demand. Further, reductions in output would be reflected in incomes thus completing a vicious circle.

But the story continues. If economic expansion depends upon prospects of larger profits, the increased employment of men and capital contributes greatly to the realization of these prospects. During the early twenties, increased activity was accompanied by large gains in net earnings. Before long, the prices of equities were correspondingly revised; each increase in income was quickly reflected in advances of capital values. In fact, as the New Era approached its end, intense trading in stocks led to the establishment of a level of prices that could have been warranted only by a sustained acceleration in economic activity. But key industries gave evidence of a retardation in their rate of growth and new industries failed to appear. The optimism of the stock market began to waver, for reduced profits were the certain accompaniment of declining trends in production. A readjustment of capital values was in order. Once in process, the revision of paper values intensified the disintegrating influences set on foot by reductions in production. Shrinkages in capital value doubtless proved a serious drag upon spending but, more important, they seriously affected the attitudes and activities of bankers.

Throughout the twenties, the banks by increasing their loans and investments added considerably to the money supply. By making available additional supplies of capital at moderately low prices, with standards conspicuous for their laxity, the banks doubtless intensified the expansion of the economy. The rapid decline in stock-market prices during the fall of 1929 ushered in a radical revision of capital values, a readjustment that left the banks highly vulnerable. Many loans on securities could not be liquidated or only at substantial losses. In the mad scramble for liquidity, total loans shrank and the money supply contracted. As the quantity and velocity of bank deposits declined, the downward revision of prices was speeded; the future became more dark. The new pessimism, not unlike the old optimism, was able to feed on itself. So the process continued.

The expansion of the twenties had within it the seeds of its own contraction, but it was a contraction well disguised. Since the last decade of the nineteenth century, the economy of the United States had progressed at a rapid rate with only the most occasional interruption. True, the postwar depression was intense, but it was also short-lived. For almost three decades the real incomes of rich and poor alike mounted rapidly; small wonder that the signposts heightened the prevailing confidence. In light of this tradition, the New Era can easily be appreciated. Yet contemporary observers who failed to appreciate it had ample opportunity to study the strategic variables. The striking expansion of the construction and automobile industries did not take place in secret; nor did newspapers conspire to hide the boom in real estate and the gyrations of the stock market; finally, imperfect as they were, banking statistics indicated the trends in money and credit.

Clearly, the rate of growth of key industries would slacken; clearly, such a development would adversely affect profits; clearly, the banks would reduce their loans. Yet, not so clearly. In February, 1929, upon the basis of an exhaustive report by experts, a distinguished group of industrialists and bankers concluded that "our situation is fortunate, our momentum is remarkable."

Part Four

SENESCENCE OF THE ILLUSION

CHAPTER VII

THE DEPRESSION

DURING the nineteen twenties, the economic expansion of the United States was subjected to careful and detailed analyses. Many were the theories that emerged to explain not only the prevailing prosperity but also to estimate the potentialities for its survival. Although the economy ran into trouble in 1924 and again in 1927, in each case the disturbance was minor. In the fall of 1929, the signs were more ominous; the decline in stock prices was as rapid as it was severe. Though the passage of every month presented increasing evidence of the cessation of economic expansion, the future was shrouded in darkness. One fact was, however, obvious: the doctrines of economic stability engendered by the prosperity of the twenties did not give way; they were made of sterner stuff. Ingrained in the minds of the mass, they were immune to pressure from the facts.*

* One is reminded of George Moore's magnificent story *The Brook Kerith*, in which Paul in flight to Rome seeks refuge among the Essenes, to whom he relates his mission. Among the members is Jesus, who since his rescue from the cross many years ago, has been without news of the city. Horrified to learn that the people are being led astray by the preaching of the resurrection, Jesus cannot bring himself to persuade Paul that there was no miracle, for he fears that Paul's mind will snap. After saving Paul's life, Jesus remarks in parting: "But seek not to understand me. Thou canst not understand me and be thyself; but Paul, I can comprehend thee, for once I was thou."

THE ILLUSION OF ECONOMIC STABILITY

There can be little doubt that to the majority of the business community the collapse of the New Era came as a shock. But if retardation in the rate of growth of the automobile and construction industries was indeed inevitable, this amazement is difficult to appreciate. One must remember, however, that from the end of the Civil War until the end of the New Era the industrial sector of the economy had progressed at an astonishing pace. Conservative estimates indicate that the average annual rate of increase in the physical volume of production was approximately 4 per cent—despite the fact that almost every industry suffered a retardation in its rate of growth, several could not escape absolute declines, and a few became extinct. Moreover, the advances in aggregate production were occasionally interrupted, especially in the seventies and the nineties of the last century, but the recession from the peak of the expansion seldom exceeded 20 per cent. After the turn of the century, the development was more regular. Upset in 1907, erratic just before the outbreak of the war, disorganized during the liquidation of 1920-21, the economy could nevertheless boast of three decades of relative stability.[1]

The annals bear witness that the entrepreneur was justified in schooling himself to an expanding economy. True, capitalistic enterprise reacts to profits, not to the physical volume of production; the individual businessman studies a limited number of forces that impinge directly upon his activities; he is little concerned with the general dynamics of the economy. Yet, his specific reactions are always limited by general tendencies, for

144

profitability depends so largely upon an expanding market. For sixty and more years, total production had been noticeably increasing, with deflections few and far between. After the severe depression of the nineties, business was remarkably free of prolonged stresses and strains. What little caution survived was dispelled by the startling developments of the New Era, an era that promised to double the "physical income of the average citizen within 29 years." During the twenties, the physical volume of manufactured goods increased 40 per cent and the annual fluctuations in aggregate output were small. As the twenties drew to a close, the business community, confident if not smug, failed to appreciate signs of warning. To discover the new, with concepts born and reared by the old, is always difficult. Imbued with an intense optimism, the economy paid little regard to the recession in construction that appeared as early as February, 1928. By the turn of the year, it became increasingly clear that the profits of the automobile industry might fail to match their previous records; yet confidence was little shaken. Although it was commonly recognized that the expansion in business was in part dependent upon foreign trade, the evidence of strains in England and Germany were slighted. Finally, when the Public Service Commission of Massachusetts, fearful of the prevailing structure of capital values, denied a large utility permission to split its stock, only a minority of the business community appreciated the implications. But with the passage of every additional month, depressive factors increased. In October, they were sufficient to force a radical liquidation in the stock market.[2]

THE ILLUSION OF ECONOMIC STABILITY

Wall Street, darling of the New Era, fell upon evil days. The majority of her admirers were greatly upset, for they learned of a sudden that they were considerably less wealthy than they had believed. A rude awakening, yet one that the more puritanical viewed as mild retribution for the orgy of speculation. For instance, Professor Fisher argued that the decline of 26 billion dollars in listed values "so full of sound and fury, signifies little." Since only one per cent of all income receivers had a total income in excess of 9,000 dollars per annum, there was every reason to believe that the majority of the population had no interest in the vagaries of the stock market. Although the liquidation might result in a greater concentration of ownership and wealth, its incidence upon production and consumption would not be great. So the story ran. Occasionally the theme would be slightly altered: "healthy liquidation"; "My only fear is the fear of fear"; "business fundamentally sound." The historically minded derived much comfort from the fact that the prelude to the depression of 1920-21 had not reoccurred; the price level had failed to rise during the New Era, and speculation in inventories had been more or less avoided.[3]

Despite tiresome repetition to the contrary, the financial and economic could not be kept asunder. Revision in security prices followed upon the accumulation of evidence that business activity was contracting. Only an optimist could hope that the collapse in security prices would not further depress business; but in 1929, the country was still basically optimistic. True, by November, 1929, indices of production and trade left something to be desired, for industrial production had been falling slowly but steadily since June; the total decline amounted to about 12 per cent. The value of construction contracts awarded that had been seeking lower levels for more than a year, suddenly dropped an additional 15 per cent between the middle and the end of 1929. However, the level of retail trade and factory employment held up rather well. The interruption to the expansion of the economy was disappointing but not disconcerting; at least not badly so, for every mature industry has, at one time or another, suffered declines in production. The rapid fall of stock-market prices did little to relieve the picture, but the strong optimistic tradition was a bulwark against morbid expectations and rapid contraction.[4]

In the past, even the most prosperous concern could not escape curtailing the employment of its men and machines in response to periodic declines in sales. During the New Era, a group of representative firms strove valiantly to stabilize their operations, a process in which they secured a high degree of success. The weakening of the market in the fall of 1929 led them to fall back upon the techniques of stabilization that had served them so well in recent years. Implicit was the assumption that the contraction in business would be transient.

Many entrepreneurs looked askance at the indiscriminate dismissal of men, and communal pressure bolstered these humanitarian sentiments. Moreover, in many businesses working capital was more than ample, for the large profits of the preceding years had not all been disbursed or reinvested. However, the determining factor

147

in continuing production in face of a decline in sales was the conviction, founded on experience, that such action might prove profitable.

When conditions took a turn for the worse toward the end of 1929, the output of many corporations was placed in warehouses rather than in stores of retailers or in homes of consumers. But even large warehouses fill rapidly. Before long, an important manufacturing corporation found itself with 80,000 refrigerators on hand. Excess supplies of a staple like soap could also prove embarrassing; even canned and packaged food accumulated with lightning speed. Although the tie-up of capital in large inventories was costly, more serious were the losses from price declines. During the New Era, savings from a heightened regularity in production and employment were seldom threatened or annihilated by depreciation in inventories. Only after many months of costly experimentation, did industry cease manufacturing for stock.[5]

Among the other prominent techniques employed during the twenties to cope with seasonal fluctuations, were price concessions; early orders were typically offered a discount of several per cent. After the collapse of the stock market in the fall of 1929, many concerns attempted to overcome the increasingly sclerotic condition of business by utilizing this efficacious method. But without result. The downward trend in the general level of prices, that gained momentum with every month, reduced the advantages of small price differentials; with the opening of the season, basic prices were frequently below those paid on early orders. Moreover, price protection, which had usually been thrown into the bargain during the twenties in order to increase the number of forward commitments, became intolerably expensive. Nor was it always advisable after 1929 to postdate bills on early orders, for the number of bankruptcies was on the increase. Yet the limitations of these several techniques were by no means obvious. Only after months of experimentation, only after losses had begun to mount, were the old techniques discarded.[6]

Fillers likewise tell an interesting story. In order to secure the more regular employment of men and machines, many concerns during the New Era manufactured minor items in off-seasons. As business declined in the fall of 1929, the introduction of new products was speeded. Once again, history failed to repeat itself. Although the majority of concerns had found fillers highly profitable during the twenties, the reverse was true after 1929. The decline in the general level of business activity sharpened competition considerably; each concern was intent upon holding its position. Concentration upon one's major line left little scope for merchandising new articles. A few corporations succeeded in face of these serious obstacles, but many found failure the reward for sallies into the unknown. In fact, the rapid shrinkages in national income turned some profitable fillers into liabilities.[7]

The stabilization movement had its roots in a widespread desire to reduce fluctuations in employment. During the twenties, several concerns that had been unable to adopt more complicated methods succeeded in part by increasing the weekly hours of work in busy periods and reducing them in slack seasons. Moreover, laborers were trained for multiple jobs so that they could be shifted as production peaks came and went. After business turned down in the fall of 1929 much attention was devoted to keeping the work force intact. The parallelisms with the New Era were slight, however, for the average work week was frequently reduced from 48 to 32 hours, sometimes to 24 hours. Stabilizing employment may have suggested spreading the work, but that exhausts the similarity.[8]

This short survey of the experiences that befell the individual concern when it employed after 1929 the techniques of stabilization developed before 1929 illustrates how the future is always victimized by the past. Success is usually its own justification, especially in a competitive economy. Small wonder, therefore, that the price level had to drop many points, and the level of business contract appreciably, before the limitations of the techniques became clear to all. Time must pass before the new can be clearly delineated from the old. Long after the stability of the economy had been upset, the ideas engendered by the prosperity of the twenties continued to play a prominent role. The history of the individual concern bears testimony thereto, but the evidence from the economy at large is more weighty.

By December, 1929, it was clear that the collapse of the stock market was intimately related to declines in production and employment. Most noticeable was a shrinkage of 20 per cent in industrial production during the preceding six months and a marked, though less intense, reduction in factory employment and payrolls. Despite constant reiteration that business was fundamentally sound, shortly before Christmas, President Hoover believed it advisable to formulate an emergency program. It had a threefold objective: to maintain the prevailing scale of wages so that the basic stream of purchasing power would not be diminished; to ensure a policy of easy money; to hasten the expansion of new construction, especially of new industrial equipment, for in truth, this was the "great balance wheel of stability."[9]

The President obtained promises of wholehearted cooperation, and soon the promises began to be fulfilled. Under the stimulus of purchases by the railroads and public utilities, industrial production climbed 9 per cent during January and February. By April, there seemed reason to believe that the worst of the disturbances, financial and economic, were at an end. Security prices had recovered 15 per cent from their November low, and industry was at a level 10 per cent higher than at the turn of the year. Factory employment and payrolls, however, presented evidence more confusing than confirmatory.

The advance proved abortive. After April, the indices began a renewed decline. The stimulation derived from the expansion programs of the railroads and utilities was insufficient to overcome the continued lethargy of the automobile industry and general construction. Moreover, it became increasingly clear that new trouble was about to develop. During the precipitous collapse of security prices, commodity prices had declined but slightly. Long years of stability and their resistance to contagion from

the stock-market collapse led to the belief that the economy would be spared any serious drop in them. By June,
this hope, like so many others, was forced to give way
before the facts. True, the commodity markets avoided
spectacular liquidation; the recession was of a creeping
variety. But the index of commodity prices in June,
1930, was 10 per cent below that for June, 1929, and the
index of farm prices had dropped 14 per cent. These
developments seriously impaired the purchasing power
of the rural population; but worse, they enhanced the
prevailing uncertainty about the future. Speculation
thrives on uncertainty; not so business. The trends in
employment and payrolls indicated the insufficiency of
President Hoover's program: in June, 1930, almost 15
per cent fewer people were employed by industry and
the total wages paid out were almost 20 per cent less than
twelve months previously.[10]

Although the passage of every day presented increasing evidence that the belief in enduring prosperity, so
common during the late twenties, was founded on fancy
rather than on fact, the attitude engendered by the New
Era died slowly.

Characteristic of the New Era was its approach to the
remuneration of labor. Despite the classical postulate
of a constant struggle between capital and labor for the
products of industry, despite socialistic adherence to it,
the twenties viewed it askance. Once captains of industry
discovered that wages were the major source of purchasing
power, they applauded the high price for labor. For profits
depended primarily upon the volume of sales, which in turn

152

depended upon the income of consumers. As the expansion of the twenties grew apace, wages rose considerably in excess of their prewar and postwar levels, a trend that greatly facilitated the emergence of the high-wage doctrine of prosperity. As the New Era came to an end, the public was thoroughly wedded to the doctrine, despite its many imperfections. Immediately after the collapse of the stock market, Henry Ford, an early convert and an able proselyter, stated: "Wages must not come down, they must not even stay at their present level; they must go up." The majority of employers were less dogmatic; nevertheless, President Hoover received widespread support in his efforts to keep wage rates unimpaired. The proof can be found in the data.[11]

The average hourly earnings of manufacturing labor amounted to 59 cents in 1929; 1930 saw no change, and 1931 recorded a loss of only 2 cents. Not until 1932 did the figure drop to 50 cents. Hourly earnings of anthracite-coal miners failed to decline throughout the depression, and employees of Class I railroads actually managed between 1929 and 1931 to increase their earnings from 65 to 67 cents per hour; in 1932, the rate was reduced to 62 cents. Common labor employed on road building earned 39 cents in 1929, the same in 1930, 36 cents in 1931, and 32 cents in 1932. Less happy was the experience of bituminous-coal miners who, after suffering severe losses between 1922 and 1929 (from 85 to 66 cents), earned only 60 cents in 1931, and 48 cents in 1932. Although these figures are not exhaustive, they reinforce each other sufficiently to suggest that hourly earnings failed to decline during the first two years of the depression and that when they did decline, after midsummer of 1931, the reductions seldom exceeded 20 per cent.[12]

Hourly earnings measure the price of labor and are a clue to the power of labor; however, they shed little light upon the welfare of the laboring class, for they fail to indicate the total volume of employment or the total number of work hours. Between 1929 and 1932, the average weekly income of employed workers shows striking declines: manufacturing, 27 to 18 dollars; metalliferous mining, 30 to 18 dollars; bituminous coal, 25 to 13 dollars; nonmetallic mining and quarrying, 26 to 16 dollars. But there were branches of the economy in which labor fared much better: public utilities, 29 to 28 dollars; wholesale trade, 30 to 27 dollars; retail trade, 23 to 20 dollars; Class I railroads, 32 to 27 dollars.[13]

Differences in the profitability of industries, in the strength of labor organization, in the adoption of the spread-work device can probably explain these striking divergences. These figures relate, however, to money earnings. When allowance is made for changes in the cost of living—the index dropped about 20 per cent—the incidence of the depression upon employed labor appears less severe. Employees in anthracite coal and Class I railroads who had the good fortune to retain their jobs during the depression increased their real weekly earnings 3 and 6 per cent respectively; those in trade and public utilities fared better, for their gains amounted to 12 and 24 per cent. Less fortunate were the groups employed in manufacturing and mining, for they suffered a loss of between 15 and 30 per cent in real weekly earnings.[14]

It was unnecessary to review these data to recall that the depression was a trial and tribulation to the majority of laborers, employed and unemployed. What the statistics did reveal, however, was the maintenance of hourly earnings during the first two years of the depression and a moderate decline once the structure gave way. To interpret this experience is not easy, for the logic of capitalistic enterprise suggests that during periods of reduced activity every effort be made to reduce costs radically, and that in view of the large number of sellers and the small number of buyers such reductions are feasible. In part, the explanation may be sought in miscalculations of the business community about the length of the liquidation. Since the majority believed that the contraction of the economy would be of short duration, they made no serious effort to reduce wage rates. Fear of strikes, especially in those sectors where labor was strongly organized, helped to forestall action. In several industries, the almost complete collapse in market demand foreshadowed little relief, even from radical reductions in wage rates. Crucial were overhead rather than variable costs. But it would be a grievous error to slight completely the influence of prevailing opinion. Throughout the New Era, the majority became convinced of the virtues of high wages; more important, the belief became widespread that high wages were the cornerstone of prosperity. Small wonder that President Hoover sought to keep the wage structure intact and that his efforts were in large part successful.

Only after several years of deepening depression was the high-wage doctrine attacked. When the venturesome Mr. Wiggin suggested that a lowering of wage rates was an essential prerequisite for recovery, he received little overt support. Those who joined his cause did so secretly. Such is the power of the idea.

In addition to the behavior of wages, the New Era paid particular attention to the behavior of prices. Belief in the stability of the economy was greatly strengthened by small fluctuations in wholesale prices. Although it was generally recognized toward the end of the twenties that the prices of equities were advancing at a suspicious rate, much comfort was derived from the failure of commodity prices to advance. In fact, after the stock-market collapse in the fall of 1929, encouragement was found in the continued stability of many prices. Quiescence during the New Era was, however, no guarantee of tranquillity during the depression. True, panic was avoided but not severe liquidation. In February, 1933, the index of all commodity prices stood 40 per cent below the level for July, 1929. Nothing was more difficult to anticipate during the depression years than this creeping decline in wholesale prices. History and theory conspired to obscure the markings; for seven years after 1922, annual variations had been slight; further, despite the speculative frenzy of the latter twenties, trading in commodities had been restrained.[15]

Although the selling prices of manufactured goods declined slowly during the New Era, large sectors of industry associated prosperity with stable prices. In fact, throughout the twenties much time and effort were devoted to ensuring a high degree of price stability. As business declined, there was, therefore, little inclination to experiment with lower prices even though such a move appeared promising. In light of their expectations that the depression would be short-lived, many concerns were unwilling to alter a price structure of long standing. The absorption of additional losses would be compensated for by enlarged profits that were certain to accompany a business revival. Once prices were lowered, it might prove impossible to raise them at a later date. The maintenance of prevailing prices was facilitated by the comparatively liquid position of industry and its marked freedom from indebtedness to the banks. The pressure to convert assets into cash (strong in the depression of 1920-21) was generally absent. Although one could easily exaggerate the influence of the New Era upon the price policy of the depression, there is good reason to believe that the naïve identification of price stability with a balanced economy, so typical of the twenties, delayed and limited price reductions after 1929.[16]

Prices march when costs command. The widespread gratification with stable prices during the twenties was a reflection of the widening differential between unit costs and unit selling prices. Between 1929 and 1931, the selling price per unit of manufactured goods declined 22 per cent. During this same period, the cost of materials dropped even more quickly—26 per cent—while labor costs per unit receded only 13 per cent. In the face of a declining volume of sales, overhead costs per unit advanced approximately 15 per cent. Profits per unit did not emerge, for the decline in selling prices exceeded that in costs. During the latter part of the depression (1931-33), the selling price per unit of manufactured goods dropped 34 per cent from the 1929 base and the cost of materials showed a slightly more rapid decline of 37 per cent. Labor costs were more rigid, though at the end of the depression they were 25 per cent less than at the peak of the New Era. Most striking was a reduction of 22 per cent in the average overhead costs per unit of product between 1931 and 1933.[17]

Throughout the depression, overhead costs were the center of attention. The much shorter liquidation of 1920-21 had illuminated the role of fixed costs in a modern economy. In fact, the stabilization movement of the twenties aimed to ensure that technology be the life, not the death, of modern capitalism. During the New Era, expenditures for plant and equipment mounted rapidly, but the large increases in total demand were more than sufficient to keep industry from losing its balance. With the contraction in business activity after midsummer of 1929, trouble loomed ahead. Since failure to make allowance for depreciation, obsolescence, and experimentation could only result in bankruptcy, the majority of large corporations set their prices, whenever possible, to cover fixed as well as variable costs. Such had been their practice for many years, a practice they continued to observe after 1929. As long as the prospect remained that the heights of the New Era would shortly be regained, deviations from the procedures of old were avoided. But as sales continued to decline, prices were driven increasingly to an out-of-pocket basis and in the depth of the liquidation to a figure not infrequently below variable costs. During the early months of the depression, price competition was more or less kept in check by trusted methods; but as disorganization swept all before it, protection of one's position, irrespective of costs, became the guiding principle.[18]

Though prices not infrequently fell to variable costs and below, demand failed to increase. The failure of labor costs to decline radically combined with a lower efficiency of production to keep variable costs high; a factory geared to 2,000 units per day could not prevent a rise in fabricating expenses when only 200 units were manufactured. During the last frenzied rush for liquidity in 1932, no price was, upon occasion, low enough to stimulate demand.[19]

The influence of the New Era upon the cost structure of the depression was evidenced on two fronts. First, the prosperity of the twenties encouraged the most cautious accountancy; with few exceptions, selling prices covered overhead costs by a comfortable margin. When business declined, every effort was made to force the small number of units to carry the total burden of overhead costs. Second, the comparatively small reductions in labor costs reflected the survival of the high-wage doctrine of the twenties.

The more rapid drop in selling prices than in costs placed industry in a weakened position; to add to its trouble, total demand contracted rapidly. Profits shrank disastrously. In 1929, the net income of all corporations amounted to approximately 8 billion dollars. During the first year of the depression, industry barely managed to keep out of the red, for aggregate profits totaled only a little more than one billion dollars. In 1931, a net deficit of more than 3 billion dollars was accumulated, and in the following year the net loss approximated 5½ billion dollars.[20]

During the New Era, the rise in profits stimulated the rise in the value of equities; in addition, anticipations of still greater earnings accelerated the advance in capital values. Economic expansion and the capitalization process worked hand in hand. Hence, as profits disappeared with the onset of the depression and losses took their place with its intensification, the price of equities could not withstand radical readjustment. Between September, 1929, and December, 1932, the value of securities on the New York Stock Exchange shrank approximately 80 per cent. A tremendous decline, but not difficult to appreciate when one recalls that in 1932 only four industries were able to earn profits—public utilities, foods, tobacco products, and chemicals. Moreover, there was good reason to believe that the deflation was far from ended; in fact, it might have no end short of universal insolvency.[21]

Since corporations paid out during the depression moneys earned in previous years, the 8½ billion dollar deficit accumulated during the two years 1931 and 1932 understates the weakened position of industry. Corporate losses for 1930-32 totaled almost 20 billion dollars. This radical change in fortune and prospect was recognized and appraised by the stock market; not so by industry itself. During the first year of the depression, the net capital assets of all corporations (excluding finance, real-estate, and service companies) actually increased from approximately 95 to 98 billion dollars, in largest measure a reflection of the expansion in public utilities. By 1932, a decrease of 10 per cent had taken place. Allowing for customary depreciation and depletion accounts as well as for new investment, the total "write-off" amounted to approximately 9 billion dollars. Between 1931 and 1934 a sample of 500 large industrial companies showed that 27 went into receivership and 12 others defaulted on fixed indebtedness; together these concerns had controlled in 1929 about 5 per cent of the invested capital of the entire group. The auctioneer's gavel received considerable wear and tear after the collapse of the New Era; commercial failures were 50 per cent greater in 1932 than they had been in 1929. Between 1930 and 1933, the cumulative excess of liabilities over assets of defaulting concerns totaled more than one billion dollars.[22]

Yet readjustment of capital values was strikingly small. In part, the increasing recourse to the stock market during the latter years of the New Era, not only for new capital but also for refunding, can explain the small number of industrial failures. At the beginning of the twenties, bonds were the backbone of industrial financing, but in the latter part of the decade as much as 75 per cent of the new capital requirements of industry was obtained through the sale of stocks. Moreover, one need but recall the large refinancing operations of the United States Steel Corporation and the Anaconda Copper and Wire

Company to realize the increasing emancipation of American industry from fixed indebtedness. The bonded debt and mortgages of all corporations other than finance, real-estate, and service companies were as large in 1932 as at the end of the New Era.[23]

Although capital assets were voluntarily reduced during the depression, when account is taken of the severe fall in prices and the uncovering of large amounts of obsolescence, the total reduction appears modest. Since assets were doubtless written up during the twenties, the hesitancy to write them down during the depression appears anomalous. It is important to emphasize, however, that the majority of the business community did not consider the New Era unstable; nor did they doubt that the recession would be of short duration. Hence, they tarried before readjusting. Their large cash balances and their freedom from bank indebtedness encouraged their resistance, nor were their fixed obligations heavy. In addition, a tax policy that emphasized "normal depreciation" contributed its mite to staying the revaluation of assets. Finally, the increasing separation of management from ownership in modern corporate life proved a substantial hindrance. Although management frequently desired a reduction in the capital structure, the board of directors was seldom in agreement, for it feared that stockholders might view the request as proof of inefficiency.[24]

Since competition was not regulated by figures on the balance sheet, the failure to revise book values must not be exaggerated. As the depression deepened, prices paid scant respect to overhead costs, yet the majority of cor-

162

porations could not make their peace with the new reality. This failure to alter the balance sheet insured that profit and loss statements would make dismal reading. If capital structures had been revised, prospective profits could more easily have appeared. Now it must not be forgotten that action in the present depends greatly upon expectations of the future. But there was an extreme reluctance on the part of the business community to admit, even in 1932, that the New Era had passed into oblivion. Neither the action of the stock market, which wrote down the value of shares by 80 per cent, nor the intense liquidation in the banking system was sufficient to convince the recalcitrants.[25]

The depression abounded in false hopes, but none was more tragic than the faith in the banking mechanism. The Federal Reserve System had carried the country through the World War; it had kept the liquidation of 1920-21 from degenerating into a panic; it had been able to facilitate the expansion of business during the New Era; and it had been instrumental in turning the tide in 1927. High in President Hoover's emergency program of December, 1929, was the promise of easy money. In fact, before the turn of the year, the discount rate was reduced from 6.25 to 5 per cent, whence it continued to drop, with only occasional reversals, until it reached in December, 1932, a low of 1.25 per cent. However, the Federal Reserve System made no strenuous effort during the first two years of the depression to implement this program of easy money by large-scale purchases of government bonds. Unfortunately, its freedom of action was considerably limited by the necessity of pursuing contradictory aims: to maintain the gold standard and at the same time to stem the liquidation of bank deposits. Not until the passage of the Glass-Steagall Act in February, 1932, could the System escape the dilemma of undermining the gold standard by protecting it. Buffeted and beaten by an economic collapse of unparalleled severity, the System failed to utilize all its resources; moreover, it was slow to take advantage of the assistance offered it by the Glass-Steagall Act. Several months passed before government bonds were purchased in substantial amounts.[26]

The monetary policy of the Federal Reserve System during the depression fulfilled only formally President Hoover's promise of easy money. The combined strain of large exports of gold in the fall of 1931 and the rise of more than one billion dollars of money in circulation during the year adversely affected the reserve balances of member banks. Possibly an omnipotent group of monetary experts in the employ of a dictator could have minimized the consequences, but the members of the Federal Reserve Board were not omnipotent and the United States was not a dictatorship.

The consequences were indeed doleful. In December, 1929, total deposits of all banks amounted to 55 billion dollars; in December, 1932, they were approximately 41 billion dollars. This decline of 25 per cent was brought about by a shrinkage in the total loans and investments from 59 to 45 billion dollars. Since investments of all banks increased during the depression from 16½ to 18½ billion dollars, loans bore the entire brunt of the liquidation.[27]

Reduced activity in the stock market accounted for a sizable portion of the total reduction in bank loans. At the time of the crash, member bank loans to brokers in New York City totaled about 2 billion dollars, and at the end of 1932 the figure had shrunk to 350 million dollars; loans to brokers outside of New York City were likewise radically reduced (from 950 to 250 million dollars); member bank loans to customers secured by stocks and bonds declined approximately 3 billion dollars. The downward trend in security prices forced a readjustment in the attitudes of the public and the banks toward Wall Street.[28]

Although the banks increased their loans on urban real estate rapidly during the New Era—in 1929, they probably held a total in excess of 10 billion dollars—the decline during the depression was very slight, probably not greater than 10 per cent. Clearly, if opportunity had offered, this reduction would have been considerably greater.[29]

In addition to the substantial reduction of all loans connected with security trading, the most radical decline occurred in commercial loans; between October, 1929, and December, 1932, "otherwise secured and unsecured loans" of all member banks declined from 12 to 6 billion dollars. It must again be emphasized that categories are but a first approximation, for the avowed purpose and the actual utilization of a loan are frequently different.[30]

Nor does this end the story. The striking contraction in bank loans and bank deposits was accompanied by an intense reduction in the exchange velocity of remaining deposits—in 1929, demand deposits outside of New York

City turned over 41 times per annum; in 1932, the comparable figure was 25. Worse still was the fact that although income velocity had failed to advance markedly during the New Era it fell substantially during the contraction in business activity.[31]

To review the depression without becoming impressed by the large declines in the supply and turnover of money is well-nigh impossible, though to explain the depression solely in terms of money would be preposterous. The study of the New Era suggested that the behavior of money facilitated and intensified the expansion of the economy; it would probably not be far from the mark to maintain that the contraction in business that set in during the latter part of 1929 and continued thereafter for more than three years was made the more severe by the actions and reactions of the banking system.

The whole alone gives meaning to the part. Although it would be a herculean task to deal adequately with the forces that determined the depression—surely economic forces could not tell the entire story—it might prove feasible to trace the major outlines. Statistical records suggest that the New Era came to an end before the winter of 1929. But eras never come to an end. Though their unity dissolves, fragments survive. Greece is still with us; so is the New Era.

Precipitated by the pronounced retardation in the rate of growth of the construction and automobile industries, hastened by the collapse of the stock market, the depression was much intensified by the contraction in bank assets and deposits. During the first year of the depression, despite large payments from reserve funds, there was a reduction of more than 6 billion dollars in aggregate income payments to individuals. To conclude that a shrinkage of only 7 per cent was not severe is more reasonable than reasoned. For it must be recalled that the output of capital goods is directly influenced by the rate of increase in the demand for the finished products manufactured by capital goods. Stability in total monetary demand would have brought strain to the capital-goods industries; hence small shrinkages could not fail to cause serious stress. Since these industries depended upon new investment, and since new investment had almost reached a standstill, they were sorely stricken. Nor could the other sectors remain healthy. By the end of 1931, the economy was badly diseased.[32]

The logic of conventional economic theory suggests that, unlike a period of expansion which may exhaust itself, contraction once begun need halt only at the brink of complete destruction. Experience suggests otherwise. In all matters social, experience is untrustworthy but it may well be preferred to logic. In the past, the economy had never failed to overcome depressive factors though it is true that the last intense and prolonged decline in production and employment had occurred as long ago as in the nineties of the last century.

But logic and experience each suggest that recovery must await the emergence of prospective profits. It has been pointed out that if, upon a contraction in business activity, all prices were immediately readjusted, the depression could be halted almost before it got under way.

But habits of thought and action change slowly; moreover, obstinacy frequently pays. Hence, unless an economy is fortunate enough to be bolstered by a demand from nascent industries at home, so powerful that they can grow despite the unfavorable environment, or by a demand from foreign sources, so determined that it will not be gainsaid by the prevailing pessimism—unless an economy receives such support, many and difficult adjustments must be undertaken before profits can once again appear on the horizon.[33]

After the collapse of the New Era, significant new industries failed to emerge, and foreign conditions were highly unfavorable. Hence, the economy was confronted by the most difficult task of readjusting without assistance; in fact, in the face of considerable resistance. Although the prosperity of the twenties was now a thing of the past, much of the New Era survived. As frequently happens, the survival of the traditional was a questionable asset.

With the rapid revision in the prices of equities after the fall of 1929 and the cumulatively large decline in wholesale prices, the reemergence of profits depended, in the first instance, upon radical declines in costs and capitalization. But the dead hand of the past was ever present. The recognition showered by the New Era upon the doctrine of high wages resulted in keeping the wage structure more or less untouchable during the first two years of the depression. Further, the twenties witnessed the marked growth in many sectors of the economy of a price policy impressed by the virtues of stability. When business began to contract, many prices remained immovable, for there was no tradition of experimentation—rather the reverse. Not until the pressure from declining activity became intense did the prices of many industrial products give way. Moreover, the belief in the basic stability of the New Era was so ingrained that, despite overwhelming evidence uncovered by the depression, the capitalization of industrial property was but slightly revised.

To suggest that the theories of economic stability which survived the collapse of the New Era influenced the course of the depression does not imply that, in the absence of these theories, the economic developments of the early thirties would have been radically different. Trade unions would assuredly have striven to maintain wage rates; loath to increase the risks of insolvency, corporations would have shied clear of experimenting with lower prices; directors would never have been in a hurry to acknowledge their mistakes by revising capital values. But the potent ideology of the New Era assuredly reinforced these resistances to liquidation.

An economy cannot enjoy the benefits of competition and at the same time look with envy upon the techniques that are part and parcel of a controlled system. Autocratic power to enforce readjustments might well have brought relief, but autocratic power is alien to unplanned economy. It has never been proved on paper, and it has obviously never been proved in fact, that a more drastic readjustment of wages, of prices, or of capital values—even one so drastic as to necessitate the aid of machine guns—would have permitted profits again to emerge. It is no idle theory but a stark fact that in 1932 captains of finance—the

Brahman caste of industrial capitalism—sought escape from the tenets of their own creed. Fearful, intimidated—in fact, panic-stricken—they could no longer face the consequences of liquidation.* Contrite and suppliant, they appealed to President Hoover, who in sympathetic understanding of their plight and the plight of the country at large, created the Reconstruction Finance Corporation. Another stark fact is that, after patiently enduring the consequences of liquidation for three years, the American public in a free election voted a mandate to a candidate who promised to leave no stone unturned in bringing the processes of contraction to a halt. By one method if not by another, the glorious heights of the New Era were to be regained.

---

* Although the theory and the facts are woefully inadequate, there can be no doubt that during the last century the subsistence economy has been increasingly displaced by the money economy, so that today only a small part of our population can remain unaffected by fluctuations in money values. It has been estimated that the ratio of net liquid claims to national wealth has risen from 15 per cent in 1890 to 40 per cent in 1930. Foreclosures of Western farms may precipitate the collapse of a Midwest mortgage company, which in turn may weaken an Eastern insurance concern, and finally endanger the annuities of a Southerner. The inability of modern capitalism to suffer radical losses may result in a failure to earn substantial profits.

CHAPTER VIII

THE NEW DEAL

A S THE election of 1932 approached, the country was sorely stricken. Compared with the rates of the last days of the New Era, industrial production had shrunk more than 50 per cent; factory employment showed an even greater contraction; construction had almost ceased. Although more than 1,000 banks had failed in 1930 and more than 2,000 went under in 1931, closures continued apace during 1932. In all, more than 3 billion dollars in bank deposits were temporarily or permanently lost. True, general conditions improved during the fall and early winter of 1932-33, as was indicated by a rise of 10 per cent in industrial production and a concomitant though slower rise in employment and payrolls; but at the turn of the year, the signs were again unpropitious. The gains of the preceding months did not continue; rather, new declines set in. Between the beginning of January and the middle of March, another 400 banks closed with total deposits of almost a quarter of a billion dollars. These figures would have been much larger but for the fact that during this period the governors of many states established "banking holidays," a device which was originally designed to afford the weaker banks time for rehabilitation but which succeeded, on Monday, March 6, in bringing all banking activity to a stop.[1]

THE ILLUSION OF ECONOMIC STABILITY

It has been argued, especially by political partisans, that the trough of the depression was reached in midsummer, 1932, and that the revival, therefore, dates from the closing months of President Hoover's administration. This contention is not without foundation in fact, for it is true that during the autumn business revived substantially. But it is also true "that this revival faded late in the year, and that a fresh contraction reduced the volume of business to another low point in the early spring of 1933." The most detailed study reveals that "of the two troughs, that in the spring was lower. . . ." When one recalls that more than 2,000 banks, with deposits totaling more than 2,500 million dollars, were forced into receivership or liquidation by the banking holiday of March, 1933, one finds little exaggeration in President Roosevelt's statement that "the almost complete collapse of the American economic system marked the beginning of my administration."[2]

The New Deal can only be appreciated against the background of a crisis, slow in maturing, acute upon arrival, resistant to therapy. Dimmed by time, occasionally erased by design, the details are seldom recalled. Nor is the fact readily remembered that speed is of the essence in meeting emergencies: research, analysis, discussion must make way for impression, formulation, action.*

---

* The tolerance of business for radical measures during the early days of the New Deal must not be forgotten. The story is told of a meeting of important industrialists and financiers, in midsummer of 1933, at which the late George Wickersham delivered a scathing attack on the administration. His attitude was highly repugnant to the group, for it believed, to a man, that President Roosevelt was doing his best to meet an emergency, a task in which all right-thinking Americans must gladly cooperate.

Financial panic, widespread unemployment, impoverished agriculture, and disorganized industry jointly conspired to place a premium upon action. At the beginning of the depression, the cessation of expansion was viewed as temporary and of short duration; as the period lengthened, faith in the inevitable recovery was weakened but not undermined. Effort was devoted to restraining the government from directly interfering with the processes of economic readjustment. Finally, pressure became so great that President Hoover was forced to act. But his was a half-hearted policy, for he had little faith in revival under governmental aegis. In the past, banks had closed; corporations had been forced into receivership; farms had been sold at auction: yet the cathartic had always restored the patient to health. Although President Hoover was disinclined to alter the regimen in 1932, an increasing number of conservative practitioners favored the use of sedatives. They feared that the patient might succumb if the more strenuous treatment were prolonged; yet they well appreciated that the use of sedatives might result in chronic invalidism. During the last twelve months of President Hoover's administration, the belief in radical liquidation was not scrapped, but it was frequently violated. Not until the election of President Roosevelt, more correctly not until his assumption of office, was this breach between principle and practice substantially reduced. His majority signified more than a widespread dissatisfaction with the dour personality of his opponent; above all, it was a vote against the failure of the state to help in the difficult process of economic readjustment. The curative powers of liquidation were too uncertain and too painful; alternative methods might well be employed.[3]

To contend that the emergency which confronted President Roosevelt was certain to lead to precipitate action does not imply that the action was unplanned. Not even the insane use means completely unsuited to their ends. The new legislation was founded on theories, a statement that in no way precludes the possibility that the theories were inadequate or false. In reconstructing the early days of the New Deal, it must not be overlooked that each measure was forced to run the gamut of pressure groups; such is the pattern of democracy. A paper solution is one thing; a political solution is something entirely different. Though conflicting interests had to be recognized, the perplexity of the country and the prestige of the President insured the administration great latitude.

Confronted with the task of reestablishing a high level of economic activity, the reformers sought for appropriate techniques. Despite the depression, the shibboleths of stability, so popular during the New Era, were once again intoned. During the twenties, considerable emphasis had been placed upon the behavior of wages and prices; high wages and stable prices were viewed as important determinants of the prevailing expansion. In the New Deal's search for prosperity, these doctrines were venerated anew. In part, the veneration might have been founded upon expediency—much of the new legislation was in need of disguise. But there is every reason to believe that the administration was strongly convinced of the intrinsic merit of the old signposts.[4]

In the opinion of President Roosevelt, the National Industrial Recovery Act and the Agricultural Adjustment Act stood "in the first rank in the program of rebuilding America." Together with the fiscal policies, they formed the core of the New Deal. The N.R.A. was passed in the hope that "united action of labor and management" could promote under governmental sanctions and supervision the fullest utilization of our productive capacity. Its objectives were twofold: to readjust the wages and hours of labor in order to increase the purchasing power of the largest group of consumers; to modify the cost and price structure of industry in order that capital might again earn a fair return.[5]

To the President and his advisers it appeared self-evident that an increase in the purchasing power of the masses would enhance the demand for the products of industry, and thus would lead to the expansion of production and employment. To raise purchasing power was imperative. The failure of President Hoover to grapple directly with this most important problem—the Reconstruction Finance Corporation did, of course, seek to prevent shrinkages in purchasing power—suggested that the task was not easy. Since President Roosevelt hoped "to stabilize for all time the many factors which make for the prosperity of the nation," supreme efforts were warranted.[6]

In view of the fact that total labor income consistently accounts for more than 60 per cent of the total national income, it was reasonable to seek increases in purchasing power through increases in the income of labor. Since wage rates and hours of employment are the major variables determining total labor income, they were the foci of the N.R.A. Although wage rates had fallen to as low as 5 cents per hour in the depth of the depression, hourly earnings declined in general at a rate approximately equal to the decline in the cost of living.[7]

In an attempt to swell total payrolls, the N.R.A. sought to raise the wages of the most poorly paid groups by the establishment of mandatory minima. Moreover, it established maximum hours of work per week. Although the low level of economic activity had reduced the average work week of manufacturing labor from approximately 50 hours in 1929 to from 36 to 38 hours during the first quarter of 1933, it was believed that a 40 hour maximum would lead to increases in employment and payrolls. Despite the radical decline in the average hours of work per week during the depression, a sizable number of laborers continued to be employed about 50 hours per week. With the establishment of a 40 hour maximum, substantial pressure was applied to balance the reduction in weekly hours of work by increases in wage rates, and many corporations readjusted wage rates so as to split the difference between the old weekly earnings and the new. Hence, the establishment of a 40 hour maximum in the majority of codes resulted in dividing the weekly labor income among a larger number of employees—a result that contributed slightly to economic recovery by heightening the velocity of spending. When wage rates were advanced to compensate for reduction in hours, payrolls were increased; but these additions to total labor income were not great.[8]

In short, the wage rather than the hour provisions were crucial. Only if entrepreneurs substantially increased their wage payments could prosperity be reestablished. Whence were the wages to come? In 1932, all corporations had a net deficit in excess of 6 billion dollars. True, this average figure obscures the fact that many concerns were able to earn profits; however, only four industries succeeded in escaping the red. With few exceptions, the working capital of American industry was insufficient to withstand new drains. Of course, a cessation of payments to stockholders, who received, even in 1932, approximately 2½ billion dollars, might have freed funds with which to increase wages. But it is doubtful whether this reallocation would have been a major stimulus to expansion, for in the most disastrous year (1932), the aggregate payroll of industry exceeded 30 billion dollars. There was one further possibility: the banks could provide the necessary funds. However, only a gullible custodian of the public's money would increase his loans to industry at a time when the majority of corporations were unable to make both ends meet, especially if the loans were to be used to meet a rise in costs. True, the enlarged payments to labor would shortly be reflected in an enhanced demand for goods; an expanding market might increase total receipts more than total costs. The argument was not without merit, but in the spring of 1933 the banks were unable to lend on merit.[9]

Poverty has ruined many an excellent experiment. Nor can there be much doubt that the bad financial position of American industry was cause to question the high-wage method of generating prosperity. Even if there were sufficient unused balances to carry part of the load; even if the creation of additional money were feasible—even then, little could be gained by wage-raising schemes unless the advances in wages were more rapid than those in prices. President Roosevelt was fully aware of this limitation, for he emphasized at the passage of the N.R.A. that "if we now inflate prices as fast and as far as we increase wages, the whole project will be set at naught. We cannot hope for the full effect of the plan unless, in the first critical months, and even at the expense of full initial profits, we defer price increases as long as possible."[10]

The modern market reacts quickly. Hence, in the six months prior to the passage of the N.R.A. the average selling price per unit of manufactured goods had risen almost 10 per cent, while hourly wages had fallen 3 per cent. The President's warning had come too late. From the moment that the administration pledged itself to raise wages, a substantial inventory boom had been set on foot. Since costs were certain to rise, manufacturers were desirous of securing the benefits of buying cheap and selling dear. Never had business been engaged in a safer gamble.[11]

The process of codification was so slow that with prices steadily on the mount the President believed it necessary "to shorten hours, and to raise wages for the shorter week to a living basis." To this end, the President's Reemployment Agreement was promulgated in August, 1933. During the two months following its adoption, hourly wage rates advanced rapidly: in manufacturing, 20 per cent; in mining, 18 per cent; in wholesale and retail trade, 15 per cent. Nor was the rise nullified by increases in prices, an eventuality feared alike by the President and his advisers. The price advances of previous months failed to maintain themselves.[12]

To test the validity of the doctrine of high wages, it is necessary to concentrate upon the months immediately following the passage of the N.R.A. and the promulgation of the P.R.A.; for as the period lengthens, other factors increase in number and significance. It is important to recall that more than nine months passed before the majority of the codes were formally adopted. Moreover, about one third of the entire laboring force was specifically exempt from the jurisdiction of the N.R.A., and a substantial number was automatically exempt because it was employed by industries whose hour and wage standards were above the newly established minima. By July, 1934, hourly earnings were approximately 25 per cent above the low for 1933, but the greater part of this advance (18 per cent) had occurred before September, 1933. Despite increases in the cost of living, which were sufficient to cancel about one third of the average gains, hourly earnings during the last quarter of 1934 compared most favorably with those for midsummer of 1933: increases of 56 per cent in bituminous-coal mining, 33 per cent in manufacturing, 24 per cent in metalliferous mining, 19 per cent in trade, 10 per cent in public utilities, 7 per cent in anthracite-coal mining, 4 per cent in road building, 3 per cent in Class I railroads. With the exception of the last two industries, employees made substantial gains in real hourly earnings.[13]

Though an important test of the high-wage doctrine of

prosperity, the trend of real and money hourly earnings does not exhaust the evidence. Weekly and yearly earnings are likewise important. If the last quarter of 1934 be compared to midsummer of 1933, one discovers that the real weekly earnings of all laborers, bituminous coal and metalliferous mining alone excepted, were lower in the latter than in the former period. In part, the explanation must be sought in the substantial employment incidental to the short-lived production boom that preceded the passage of the N.R.A.; in part, the explanation can be found in the maximum hour provisions incorporated in the codes. During the twelve months following June, 1933, lessened production and legal limitations conspired to reduce the average work week almost 20 per cent. The fact that many employees suffered absolute declines in real weekly earnings and the further fact that the N.R.A. was at least partially responsible for this decline suggest that the ability of the higher wages and shorter hours to generate prosperity was vastly overrated. But neither weekly earnings nor hourly earnings exhaust the story: of preeminent importance are aggregate figures of employment and payrolls.[14]

These latter criteria place the N.R.A. in a much more favorable light, for total employment of manufacturing labor increased from an average of 5,700,000 in 1933 to 6,700,000 in midsummer of 1934; the advance in weekly payrolls was likewise substantial; from 98 to 125 million dollars. If the labor provisions of the codes be credited with these gains, the high-wage doctrine of prosperity must be respected, if not approved. However, the early months of the New Deal witnessed a broad fusillade upon the depressed economy, and it is therefore impossible to evaluate the specific contribution of the N.R.A. Only first approximations may be ventured. This much is certain, that the industrial boom which led to an increase in production of almost 70 per cent between March and July, 1933, was in largest measure predicated upon the higher costs that were to follow the wage-raising policies of the new administration. True, the boom was short-lived. By November, the index had again dropped to a level only 15 per cent in excess of that for March. Intensity without duration is seldom valuable, but three years of deep depression made many grateful even for small favors. The gain in morale, more particularly the gain in profits, was greatly appreciated.[15]

To admit that the policy of raising wages contributed greatly to the inventory boom of 1933, and to go farther and admit that the establishment of minimum standards helped check the effects of destructive competition, cannot establish the validity of the high-wage doctrine. After the passage of the N.R.A., wage rates were rapidly advanced and business declined; in the fall of 1934, however, when wage rates were not being changed, business revived. Clearly, the correlation between wage raising and business expansion was not high. Economic theories can seldom, if ever, be disproved by facts but if the facts do not fit, the burden of proof is on the proponent of the theory.

It has been pointed out that the high-wage doctrine of prosperity became so firmly entrenched during the New Era that it was able to survive, more or less successfully,

181

the worst depression in the entire history of the country. In search of techniques to restore prosperity, President Roosevelt was certain to stumble upon the doctrine:

> There is a clear way to reverse that process . . . (of a continuous descent into the economic hell of the past four years). . . . If all employers . . . agree to pay the same wages . . . then higher wages . . . will hurt no employer. Moreover, such action is better for the employer than unemployment and low wages, because it makes more buyers for his product. That is the simple idea which is the very heart of the Industrial Recovery Act.

Preoccupation with raising the price of labor did not imply that the administration limited its activities to this one approach. During the depression, wholesale prices dropped precipitously, a decline that reflected severe stresses in various sectors, and a decline that in turn increased these stresses. During the New Era, considerable emphasis had been placed upon the proximate identity between stability in wholesale prices and stability in the economy at large. Of course, the stability of each had proved illusory; but the evidence had been carefully disguised from 1922 to 1929, a period long enough for the doctrine of stable prices to become well entrenched. However, no reasonable man could doubt, after three years of intense depression, that stable prices, like high wages, were an uncertain guarantee of economic stability. Yet men are seldom reasonable. Nothing is more intractable than beliefs unsupported by facts. Of course, the collapse of the price level was associated with a marked deterioration in the economic position of many groups; debtors were especially hard pressed. It is not surprising therefore that President Roosevelt was particularly concerned with raising the price level. Convinced that a return to, and a stabilization at, the 1926 level were desirable, he concentrated upon the speedy achievement of his goal. Clearly debtor classes were hurt by the precipitate fall in prices, but it did not follow that they would be substantially aided by a rise. Debts are paid out of income and a rise in prices might easily entail a reduction in the purchasing power of debtor income. To many, the President's choice of 1926 as a goal was far from obvious; moreover, there were good reasons to suspect that the methods of reaching the goal foreshadowed the impossibility of maintaining one's position once the objective had been achieved.[16]

In October, 1934, the index of wholesale prices was 33 per cent in excess of the level that had prevailed at the beginning of President Roosevelt's administration. During these twenty months, it had recovered approximately half of the ground that had been lost during the depression; at the end of another twenty months, it was, however, far distant from the goal of 1926. The advance in prices during the last nine months of 1933 exceeded the gains for 1934 and 1935. But the retardation in its rate of increase was of questionable significance. Neither history nor theory would lead one to believe that a return to the price level of 1926 was an essential prerequisite for economic recovery. The doctrine of stable prices had been born in error and had been fed by illusion. If the exigencies of life demand, false doctrines can easily be transformed into sacred dogmas.[17]

THE ILLUSION OF ECONOMIC STABILITY

During the New Era, price analysts looked with favor upon the trend of agricultural prices. The breach between agricultural and industrial prices, created by the depression of 1920-21, was being slowly but steadily healed, a development that led many to believe that the prevailing prosperity was becoming ever more firmly entrenched. But the collapse of the New Era brought an end to the rapprochement. The depression was merciless to agriculture. Once again, theories died hard. Since "the purchasing power of nearly half our population depends on adequate prices for farm products," President Roosevelt was convinced that agricultural prices were an important key to general prosperity. As soon as the banking crisis was under control, he turned his attention to the plight of the farmer. Between March and July, a startling development had, however, taken place: the prices of farm products had risen 50 per cent. Because the advance occurred before the administration had time to act, one cannot conclude that it was uninfluenced by politics. Like the industrial boom, the spurt in agricultural prices discounted governmental action. After specific legislation had been enacted, the rise was interrupted. In fact, it was not until the severe drought of 1934 that prices again advanced. The drought clearly was not an integral part of the agricultural program, though the curtailment of supplies and the concomitant rise in prices were welcome aids to farmers in general, if not to the drought sufferers in particular. The improved position of the farmer since the advent of the New Deal—nobody doubts that there has been a marked improvement, though many doubt that it will last—was not solely dependent upon the trend in agricultural prices. Refinancing of farm mortgages, governmental purchases of surpluses, price guarantees, benefit payments, all contributed to the recovery of agriculture. To gauge the extent of the recovery, one need only note that agricultural income increased between 1932 and 1934 from 3 to 5 billion dollars.[18]

These gains had their price. Between 1932 and 1934, the physical volume of agricultural production declined 10 per cent; the marked increase in farm prices had unfavorable repercussions upon the cost of living; in addition to burdening specific industries and later draining the Treasury, the crop-restriction program doubtless delayed essential readjustments in our farm plant. When one recalls, however, that in 1932 many county governments were bankrupted, creditors could no longer gain protection from the law, farm strikes were on the increase—the costs of agricultural recovery appear reasonable. Although one need not agree with President Roosevelt that the rejuvenation of the farmers was a force almost without equal in turning the general contraction into expansion, the improvement of agriculture doubtless contributed to the revival of the economy.[19]

Preoccupation with raising the price of labor and agricultural commodities did not exhaust the price policies of the new administration. Interest was likewise centered upon the stabilization of industrial prices. Although competition is usually the life of trade, it can upon occasion be the death of trade. For many decades, overhead costs as a percentage of total costs had been increasing, a trend predicated upon enlarged investments in plant and equipment. Sudden shrinkages in market demand, such as as occurred in 1920-21, disclosed, however, that large-scale industry was vulnerable to intense competition. When prices drop to variable costs or below, nobody is secure. Throughout the New Era, many producers sought to keep their prices stable, and in general they were markedly successful. In attempting to account for the exceeding good fortune of the economy at large, many industrialists found the answer in these successful efforts at stabilization. With the contraction of business activity that gained momentum after the collapse of the stock market in October, 1929, intensified efforts were made to keep price competition within limits. The tradition of cooperation and the animus against price cutting were at first able to exercise a restraining force, but under the pressure of ever-smaller markets these prejudices were forced to give way. By 1932, market prices were not infrequently below operating costs; protection of one's market position was the sole criterion. One after another of the customary limits of competition was exceeded in the struggle for survival, nor did the scuttling of standards bring relief. Rather the reverse; chaos and bankruptcy loomed on the horizon. No program of economic reform could neglect the prevailing "disorganization of industry."[20]

In the structure of the N.R.A., the elimination of "unfair competitive practices" balanced the wage and hour provisions; the support of industry was gained with the former, while the latter was bait for labor. Although industry had striven for many years to limit price competition,

186

and although in prosperous times such efforts were rewarded with considerable success, unfavorable market conditions could wreck the most elaborate plans. Worst of all, the law was a constant threat. Despite popular misconceptions, the courts had failed to nullify the antitrust laws; nor were the penalties of triple damages and a jail sentence without restraining influence. Section 5 of the N.R.A., however, specifically exempted industries operating under a code or license from the provisions of the antitrust statute. To gauge the importance of this waiver, one need but recall that 80 per cent of all codes contained provisions that directly or indirectly limited price competition. Although more than a hundred different methods were explicitly adopted, the more usual techniques were limited to uniform methods of cost accounting, open price systems, specified discount, and credit terms.[21]

The haphazard revision of the plane of competition under the aegis of codification contributed little, if anything, to the recovery of the economy. In fact, there is good reason to believe that its net contribution was negative. At first, criticism of the N.R.A. was slight, but within six months after the passage of the act Senator Nye collected 1,000 pages of testimony replete with evidence that the codes were facilitating the domination of small enterprises; that the activities of trade associations were largely directed to utilizing their new immunities to fix prices; that the consumer was increasingly at the mercy of organized minority groups.

Despite mounting criticism, the administration could not cease its vacillations on price policy; finally the Supreme Court brought the entire experiment to permanent rest. Although the suspension of the antitrust laws might originally have stimulated business, the permission extended trade groups to control prices and production was certain to be abused. Profit is always a function of exploiting opportunities, and the ability of manufacturers to cooperate offered an excellent opportunity. The interest of business groups in stable prices is not surprising; that this interest should have been intense after four years of devastating competition is likewise not surprising. The administration's belief that production and employment could be enhanced by permitting—in fact, facilitating—agreements between competitors alone is surprising. But pressure was substantial and compromise essential. If action there must be, theories can always be manufactured; more easily can they be resurrected.[22]

That the pressure was real, none can doubt. At the beginning of 1933, the wage and hour structure of many industries was seriously demoralized, a condition that gave promise of spreading. Industrial prices had reached a point that ensured losses, if not bankruptcy, to almost every sector. In addition, the phenomenal decline in agricultural prices—the major variable determining the income of farmers—endangered the entire social fabric. The general price level had dropped so far, so quickly, that all long-time contracts were in danger of nonfulfillment. Confronted with those indubitable facts and possessed of a mandate to act, the new administration strained itself to reverse the trend. Under the severe pressure of time the New Deal failed to study in detail the relations between its several recovery measures. Were they in all cases complementary or were they upon occasion contradictory? The President did not believe that the question permitted an *a priori* answer. Skeptical of theory, he proceeded empirically. To raise farm prices, restrict supplies. To raise wages and lower hours, establish minima above the prevailing standards. To eradicate intense competition, permit industry to agree on trade practices. To raise the price level, devalue the dollar.

To raise wages would add not only to the purchasing power of labor but might also add to the costs of industry and thereby place an additional impediment in the way of enlarging production and employment. To facilitate an advance in farm prices would not only enrich the farm community but it might increase the cost burden of industry and hurt the consumer. To raise the price level would permit the repayment of debts with cheaper dollars but it might also frighten investors into withholding their funds.

Time was short and the propounder of paradoxes was not in favor. The Hoover administration had been held prisoner for three years by its own fears, from which it was freed only by the election of 1932. President Roosevelt realized that relief was essential; hence, action and speed were at a premium. Standards have meaning only in time and place. A careful and detailed analysis of the economic scene prior to the formulation of a program of reform was surely desirable but it was surely impossible. Specific approaches to specific problems were the best alternative but one that invited inefficiency and error. Despite the pragmatism of the New Deal, its each and every action was supported by theory, especially by doctrines that had gained popularity during the New Era. Though the depression had liquidated the reality of the twenties, it had not succeeded in liquidating its ideology. In part, the survival can be explained by group interests: labor protected the high-wage doctrine; industry nursed the stable-price doctrine; agriculture was much concerned about parity prices; debtors were interested in a stable-price level. Stock speculation aside, the New Deal looked longingly at the New Era, a period of "fair prices," "fair wages," "fair profits"; a period when employment was full and factories were busy. The New Era had given rise to the New Economics; and though the New Era collapsed, the New Economics suffered exile but not death. During the depth of the depression, the Old Economics reestablished itself: wage-cutting, price-cutting, bankruptcy. The regime of liquidation was firmly entrenched. But the land did not find peace. The defeat of President Hoover was a defeat for the Old Economics. In search of an alternative, the new administration found the doctrines of the twenties conveniently at hand. Their resurrection was in order. In need of rationalizing actions that it could not avoid, the government paid them homage; in search of a stronger market position, important groups found them useful. But this is not the entire story. Offspring of the twenties, these doctrines were relied upon to serve as guides once a return to the twenties became the order of the day.[23]

With fits and spurts but with a persistency that overshadowed the minor lapses, the economy expanded from year to year. As the election of 1936 approached, industrial production was 80 per cent greater than it had been in the spring of 1933. Factory employment had increased 60 per cent and factory payrolls had more than doubled. The prices of farm products were almost 100 per cent greater than at the beginning of the New Deal. The stock market was likewise buoyant, for security prices had risen 250 per cent.[24] In asking the electorate for a second term, President Roosevelt summarized the achievements of his recovery program in the following manner:[25]

Are you an investor? Your stocks and bonds are up to five and six-year high levels.

Are you a merchant? Your markets have the precious life-blood of purchasing power. Your customers on the farm have better incomes and smaller debts. Your customers in the cities have more jobs, surer jobs, better jobs.

Are you in industry? Industrial earnings, industrial profits are the highest in four, six, seven years! Bankruptcies are at a new low.

These enviable records did not obscure the fact that several gains were specious, for they reflected changes in money rather than in real income. Moreover, the intractability of the relief problem illustrated that recovery was far from complete; the limited absorptive capacity of the economy for new labor was frightening. The American public was greatly impressed with the progress that had been made, however, and its overwhelming vote for President Roosevelt expressed its appreciation and confidence.

So quickly were the scars of the depression healing that

President Roosevelt was hopeful. Shortly after restoring "values to a normal and proper level," he declared, "it is our aim to maintain them at a normal and proper level. . . . Our objective for all citizens is to give permanence to employment, safety to earnings, protection to the home and a better security to the average man and his family. That can be done. You and I will carry on until it is done." The belief in enduring prosperity was resurgent. Increasingly the New Deal recalled the New Era.[26]

During the early days of the New Deal, an occasional student was upset by the parallelisms with the New Era; and as these increased, his anxiety mounted. Despite the fact that the twenties had given the lie to the high-wage doctrine of prosperity, President Roosevelt saw fit to resurrect it and assign it an important place in his recovery program. As the expansion gathered strength, moreover, the high-wage doctrine was ever more deeply respected. Although the critical observer could not gainsay the prevailing prosperity, there were ample grounds to distrust the proffered interpretations. True, the literate were forced to admit that the high-wage doctrine of the New Deal had more right to be heard than had the high-wage doctrine of the New Era. A review of the twenties illustrated that entrepreneurs possessed no mechanism to raise wages collectively nor did they possess any incentive to raise them individually, a fact borne out by the statistics which showed that, with few exceptions, wage rates had not been advanced. President Roosevelt took care to meet both objections. Yet there was reason for skepticism despite the undeniable fact that wage rates had been advanced in

192

unison during the early days of the New Deal, and despite the fact that the economy had expanded though not synchronously. During the twenties, addition to, rather than redistribution of, the available purchasing power was at the heart of the expansion. A strong presumption existed for a similar interpretation of the Roosevelt recovery. Since the expansionary factors had exhausted themselves in the twenties, the pessimists were worried about their vitality in the thirties.

Equally suspect was President Roosevelt's estimate of the contribution of agriculture to the general revival. He was doubtless correct in pointing out that "people in the manufacturing cities will find more employment at better wages if the farm families of the nation have the wherewithal to purchase manufactured goods. . . ." That agriculture improved remarkably under the solicitous care of the New Deal, none can deny; that its recovery stimulated other sectors of the economy can likewise not be denied. What may be questioned, however, is the original stimulus of this improvement. The gains in agriculture, like the gains in labor, could probably not be found in a redistribution of existing purchasing power but must be sought rather in a net addition to purchasing power. Although the majority were satisfied that the high-wage and price-parity doctrines correctly accounted for the progress of the New Deal—it must not be forgotten that these same doctrines found favor during the New Era—the depression that separated the prosperous twenties from the prosperous thirties kindled in some a strong skepticism of optimistic interpretations.

THE ILLUSION OF ECONOMIC STABILITY

A review of the twenties disclosed that the phenomenal expansion of the automobile and construction industries, the optimism engendered by their expansion, and the aid provided by increases in bank deposits offered a more reasonable interpretation of the New Era than was afforded by the high-wage doctrine of prosperity. The former approach disclosed the factors working toward expansion but it also disclosed how these same factors were likely to bring the expansion to a close. Since the New Era did collapse in the fall of 1929, a theory that could explain both the emergence and the subsidence of prosperity was surely to be preferred to one which concentrated upon the enduring qualities of prosperity.

Not out of ill will toward President Roosevelt but rather out of a wisdom born in experience, a small minority were unable to accept the high-wage and price-parity doctrines as correct interpretations of the New Deal's progress. They sought for strategic factors, but theirs was a search free from an optimistic bias. Without great difficulty, they settled upon money as the open sesame of the New Deal.

During the New Era little heed had been paid to the vagaries of the monetary mechanism. Attention had been focused upon automobiles, buildings, radios, and refrigerators rather than upon ciphers in the books of the banks. Once the New Era was no more, a superficial study revealed that a rise in bank deposits from 35 to 55 billion dollars between 1921 and 1929 was probably a factor worthy of consideration in evaluating the prosperity of the decade. In the ensuing period of decline, the dissipation of 2 billion dollars of bank deposits during the first year, 7 billion dollars during the next year, 4 billion dollars during the third, and an additional 4 billion dollars in 1933—a grand total of approximately 17 billion dollars—awakened the entire country to the implications of money. Although committed to a policy of liquidation, the Republican administration did not dare to follow the policy rigidly; hence, it permitted the federal debt to increase by 5 billion dollars, or more than 25 per cent, in a vain effort to stem the tide of financial contraction. By suasion more powerful than respectable, the banks were forced to absorb increasing amounts of short-term governmental paper, a practice that Mr. Roosevelt condemned during the campaign of 1932 as a serious drag on recovery. Less concise were his remarks on money. His advocacy of a "sound but adequate currency" led the more pessimistic to conclude that he would not hesitate to violate the *sanctum sanctorum*, of modern capitalism, though his strictures of President Hoover indicated he would shun certain techniques. Senator Glass, whose orthodoxy was beyond reproach, attempted, however, to reassure the country.[27]

Fate conspired that upon his assumption of office, President Roosevelt should be the silent partner to the most intense liquidation that the economy had ever witnessed: more than 2 billion dollars in bank deposits were seriously damaged or permanently destroyed. The requisitioning of all public holdings of gold in March, and the interdiction of its export in April, were precipitated by the President's realization that he had but two courses open to him: "to cut down the debts through bankruptcies and foreclosures . . . or else to increase property values. Obviously, the latter course was the only legitimate method of putting the country back on its feet without destroying human values." During the campaign, Governor Roosevelt had indicated that a stricter deflationary policy, especially in federal financing, might prove a real contribution to recovery. After the deflation in bank deposits that ushered in his term of office, President Roosevelt no longer viewed this approach favorably. His every action was now directed toward securing "an increase in all values": international cooperation was scorned; large-scale expenditures for relief and rehabilitation were voted; the dollar was devalued.[28]

Before many months had passed, banking statistics revealed that the drive to restore values to a higher level was well under way. On June 30, 1933, total deposits of all banks were 38 billion dollars. By the end of the year a modest rise had occurred, and in June, 1934, the figure had jumped to 42 billion dollars. The next six months witnessed a further increase of 3 billion dollars, and by the end of 1935 the total approximated 49 billion dollars. Within the course of two and a half years, total bank deposits showed a rise of 11 billion dollars, an advance unparalleled in the history of the country. The record established during the World War was broken.

This increase in deposits was predicated upon a rise of almost 6 billion dollars in the loans and investments of all banks and additions of more than 3 billion dollars in member bank reserves with the Federal Reserve System as well as an increase of almost 2 billion dollars of member bank balances with domestic banks. Most interesting is the category "loans and investments," for its breakdown suggests the strategic factors at work. While total investments mounted by 7,500 million dollars, total loans declined by almost 2,000 million. Increased holdings of government bonds can explain much. Between June, 1933, and December, 1935, member banks expanded their portfolio for governments from 6,800 to 10,500 million dollars. In addition, they held at the close of 1935 almost 2 billion dollars of bonds fully guaranteed by the government. The close correlation between governmental financing and the rise in bank deposits can be gauged by the rise of 8,500 million dollars in federal securities of member banks that was paralleled by a rise of 7 billion dollars in demand and 2 billion dollars in time deposits.*[29]

The effective money supply is always a function of two variables—quantity and velocity. During this period when the quantity of bank deposits was increasing with unparalleled rapidity, velocity failed to keep pace. Continuing the decline that had set in at the beginning of the depression, the rate of deposit turnover failed to increase

* Although spending was the strategic contribution of the government to revival, it need not have led to a rise in bank deposits and in bank holdings of government bonds. The fact that it did is, however, clear. Lauchlin Currie has recently shown—"The Economic Distribution of Demand Deposits," JOUR. AMER. STAT. SOC., June, 1938—that "unless we account for the excess of business sales over disbursements in terms of the increase in incomes due to Government spending, we will be forced to the view that . . . the savings of consumers were a negative quantity. In view of (a) the direct evidence that Government spending increased some persons' incomes and (b) the indirect evidence of saving on the part of consumers . . . the fiscal policies of the Government were causing the income of the community to be in excess of the disbursements of business to the factors of production plus the payment of taxes. . . ."

despite the renewed expansion of the economy. Uncertain of the future, entrepreneurs were not avid for new funds.

The New Deal wrought the most substantial changes in our financial life. Institutions of long standing were subjected to sudden and violent change; almost overnight, gold disappeared from the eyes of men. Radical experimentation with silver purchases; the mobilization of a tremendous stabilization fund; devaluation of the dollar; the multiplication of governmental lending agencies; the guarantee of bank deposits—this is an incomplete roll call. Political pressure forced certain of these changes; economic theorizing was at the heart of others. Conservatives were horrified at these sweeping alterations in our financial life, and many prophesied the most dire consequences. Although the future may yet prove them right, there can be little doubt that the immediate implications of this radical program were indeed slight. With one single exception, the New Deal was substantially unaffected by these developments. But the one exception is important.

It has been estimated that during the three years 1934-36 inclusive, net federal income-increasing expenditures totaled in excess of 10 billion dollars, an amount about half as great as the cumulative annual increase in national income. Since it is not unwarranted to assume that the expenditure of one new dollar may increase the national income not by one but by two dollars, the conclusion emerges that "the rise in national income in the last three or four years could be imputed almost entirely to governmental spending."[30]

To ascribe such a transcendental importance to govern-

198

mental fiscal policy does not necessarily imply approval, much less adulation. In the absence of substantial governmental spendings, recovery might have occurred; in fact, it might have been more intense and prolonged. The evidence is confusing.

There can be no doubt that in midsummer of 1932 total production and employment began to expand noticeably. In largest measure, this reversal of the contracting forces can be sought in enlarged activity of the semidurable consumers'-goods industries in addition to the revival of the automobile industry. The active shift in Federal Reserve policy was likewise encouraging. But the recovery was short-lived. With the onset of winter, the indices once again turned down, probably speeded on their way by the increasing difficulties of the banks. Nor was the political interregnum an economic asset. President Hoover was completely discredited and President-elect Roosevelt was an enigma.

Although a period of depression usually precipitates factors tending toward eventual revival—obsolescence of machinery, new inventions, reduction in inventories, revision of specific prices—it is likewise true that a period of depression, especially prolonged depression, makes such a revival increasingly difficult. Consumers' reserves can be drained to swell inactive corporation balances, the decline in output reduces the pressure to replace old plant and equipment, the radical disruption of the price level can reduce the incentives for new investment. There is no *theoretical* necessity for a revival to follow a period of liquidation until the reduction in national income has become so great as to threaten the entire social fabric. There is, however, much *historical* evidence to prove that every prior liquidation was reversed long before such a point was reached.

One might assume that at the beginning of 1933 the historical evidence would have engendered optimism. For some, it did; others were not cheered by a review of the annals. Not since the nineties had the economy been subjected to a depression of such terrific intensity; in fact, with the exception of the nineties, industrial capitalism in the United States had never known a severe depression. The seventies were not comparable, for industry then was still in its infancy, a factor of great importance in conditioning the course and conclusion of that collapse.

In reviewing the more moderate depressions one was impressed with the part that speculative investment, by increasing the stream of purchasing power, had played in turning depression into revival. New industries and new people were the foundation of speculative investment. The potential profitability of the railroads, the utilities, the automobile was sufficiently great to warrant the building of plant and equipment in advance of market sales. More important, perhaps, were the phenomenal increases in our population that afforded excellent safeguards to the speculative investor.* In estimating the possibilities of recovery from the depression that followed the collapse of the New

* The crux of the population argument is found in the contention that entrepreneurs will be less hesitant to make investments in plant and equipment if they can anticipate regular increases in population, for such increases will contribute greatly to correcting any temporary excesses in capacity.

Era, little comfort could be garnered from these sources; new industries were not in the offing and additions to our populations were modest. During the formative stages of the New Deal, many competent observers believed that the moral from history reinforced the logic of theory: recovery without governmental action was far from certain; in fact, it was highly improbable.[31]

Technological progress never ceases; hence new investment is always imminent. In frightening the investment community by financial manipulation, President Roosevelt doubtless retarded capital expenditures, though a larger measure of responsibility might be ascribed to nonfiscal measures: reform of the securities market, utility legislation, labor policy. Moreover, the introduction of large streams of purchasing power facilitated advances in prices, not all of which proved stimulating. In view of the prolonged stagnation of capital expenditures, it appears doubtful, however, whether these New Deal measures must bear more than a little blame.

Because of the low level of utilization of capacity during the trough of the depression, large increases in demand could be satisfied before pressure for plant expansion became substantial. Moreover, the intensity of the building boom during the twenties probably precluded a large expansion in construction in 1933. Undermaintenance of roadbeds and delayed replacements of equipment during the depression suggested that the railroads were potentially large customers for capital goods. So they were, but so they would remain until freed from bonded servitude. The revival of the automobile industry was the exception.

Able to move against the trend in 1932, it was greatly aided by the trend after 1933.[32]

At the beginning of the New Deal, a building boom was not incipient and the railroads were prostrate. The automobile industry was on the advance and the administration measures doubtless sped it on its way. Washington may be blamed for curtailing the probable expansion of the utilities and for increasing the difficulties of new industrial financing. Together the total might not have been small. But governmental action could not have stayed enticing speculative investments. Most probably they were absent.

The weight of evidence suggests that the economy would have waited in vain had it been forced to await in 1933 the expansion of the capital-goods industries. Except for stimulation which could have been anticipated from the revival in automobiles, the present and the near future were indeed bleak. The stimulation engendered by governmental spending must be rated highly, for the failure of capital goods to revive suggests that the new money poured out by the government was largely responsible for the general expansion of the economy. The recovery set under way by the strivings and strainings of President Roosevelt and his administration was a "consumption recovery." Durable consumers' goods carried the brunt of the advance between 1933 and 1937. New investment took place but it was "geared rigorously and narrowly, in a quite unusual degree, to the immediate requirements of consumption."[33]

To admit that economic theory recommended and political pressure dictated governmental spendings at the beginning of the New Deal does not imply that such action should have been enthusiastically undertaken or optimistically evaluated. Forced moves usually have a bad prognosis. It is not surprising therefore that many analysts viewed the spending program askance, for they felt assured that, whatever its immediate incidence, the long-run implications would be disastrous.

The collapse of the New Era had proved once again that additions to the money supply, though immediately stimulating were potentially depressing. The expansion of bank deposits during the twenties had been based upon increased loans on real estate and securities and enlarged investments in private and public bonds. To the great surprise of many, marketability was no insurance against loss. Since future expectations played the determining role in the evaluation of long-time assets, and since these expectations were subject to gross exaggeration under the pressure of group psychoses, sudden and intense revisions of prevailing prices were more or less inevitable. Once revision sets in, marketability becomes a farce, for liquid claims can only be traded; they can never be redeemed.

The New Era should have been a warning to the New Deal. Increases in bank deposits based upon increased holdings of long-time assets indicated danger. Only stable assets could have helped to quiet the anxiety. Since the assets were government bonds, President Roosevelt felt assured that the banking system was as sound as the government; no sounder. His critics foresaw more imminent trouble; even a small reduction in the price of government bonds might prove disastrous, for the undivided profits and surpluses of most banks would be insufficient to absorb the losses.

Worse still was the fact that the governmental spendings were associated with an ever-mounting federal debt. Temporary increases in the debt were one thing; constant increases something entirely different. From the beginning of the New Deal's ambitious program of fostering economic revival through governmental action, President Roosevelt reiterated that deficit financing was temporary. It was a transition stage to renewed private spendings.

In June, 1936, federal net income-increasing expenditures reached an all-time monthly high of 540 million dollars; thereafter, a rapid decline set in and by December the figure had shrunk to 300 million dollars. The total for the calendar year, 1936, however, exceeded 4 billion dollars. During the next twelve months, the rate of decline was accelerated so that in November, 1937, net income-increasing expenditures were zero. Compared to 1936, the total for the year showed a decrease of more than 75 per cent. Less radical than his critics were willing to admit, President Roosevelt lost little time in bringing the transition period to an end.[34]

Unfortunately, private spendings did not expand markedly. Corporate security issues for new capital totaled slightly over one billion dollars in 1936, an insignificant figure when one recalls that the quarterly average for 1925-29 was in excess of 1,250 million dollars. Nor did the first half of 1937 show a noticeable advance; by the end of the year, even this modest level could no longer be maintained.[35]

The stock market had foreseen neither the radical reduction in governmental spendings nor the sluggishness of private spendings. Projecting the trend of 1935-36, stock-market prices reached a high in February and March of 1937 when the index stood at 130 (1926=100), an increase of more than 60 per cent over the 1935 average. Until September, its movements were irregularly sagging; but in that month the index dropped 15 points, which was followed by another drop of 15 points in October. Probably more than in any other country, business activity in the United States is sensitive to the vagaries of the stock market, though to be sure the trend of business itself largely determines the prices of equities.[36]

The rapid and almost uninterrupted rise of industrial production during 1936 from 93 to 121 (1923-25 = 100) led in late autumn and winter to a rapid rise in costs and prices, in part engendered by a fear of shortages, in part a reflection of an active unionization drive. Although incomes in both industry and agriculture reached a high in the middle of 1937, the rate of increase was being substantially retarded, probably a determining factor in precipitating price declines in raw and semifinished products and bringing the stock market advance to a halt.[37]

The automobile industry, important in its own right, very important because of the continued stagnation of the capital-goods industries, was likewise dependent upon the rate of increase in national income, especially after four years of steady expansion. Since large numbers of old cars had been turned in, the replacement demand was noticeably slackening; new sales became therefore largely a function of conspicuous consumption, which in turn was largely a function of rising incomes. By September, 1937, the future looked bleak.

Throughout the first eight months of 1937 industrial production maintained approximately the level achieved toward the end of 1936, but the indices failed to advance. Starting in September, they commenced to decline at a rate hitherto unknown in the economic annals of the country. Nor did the spring of 1938 bring revival, though seasonal factors were sufficiently potent to halt the decline—but not before the level of physical output was almost 35 per cent below the figure of six months previously.[38]

After four years of substantial improvement in production and employment, the recovery was halted in September, 1937. Recalling 1929, only a small minority were truly pessimistic; the vast majority were reconciled to an interruption but not to a decline. The administration was clearly unperturbed. Not until "the hoped-for reemployment" of the spring failed to mature did President Roosevelt take action. Determined to avoid a repetition of the Hoover debacle, which in part could be explained by the inaction of the federal government, President Roosevelt emphasized in his message to Congress in April, 1938, that "the National Administration has promised never to stand idly by and watch its people, its business system and its national life disintegrate." Despite his dislike of additional governmental spending, his message was exclusively devoted to recommendations concerning the relaxing of credit and the renewal of income-increasing expenditures.[39]

To believe in action was intelligent; to believe in spendings was warranted; to believe in "a stabilized recovery through a steady mounting of our citizens' income and our citizens' wealth" was alone illusory.

Part V

DEATH OF THE ILLUSION

CHAPTER IX

STABILITY AND CHANGE

NO PERIOD in history can approximate, far less parallel, the rate of change in economic relations that followed the invention of Watt's steam engine. Most men viewed these changes approvingly; criticism was limited to an occasional romantic who hated the machine, or to an occasional materialist who hated the owners of the machine. But romantic and materialist alike were unable to make headway, for the standard of living of the mass was markedly on the rise and the gains of entrepreneurs were frequently phenomenal. Yet all was not gain; for during periods of business contraction and stagnation, men who depended on money wages for their daily bread were unable to obtain employment, and machines capable of producing useful goods were forced to rust because of a paucity of orders. Although the morose could indict industrial capitalism for marked inefficiency on many scores, the temperate were able to point out that no system was ever without fault. The comparative infrequency of major breakdowns led reasonable men to evidence satisfaction with the record.[1]

The balance sheet of the United States was conspicuously good. With the exception of the seventies and the nineties, prolonged depressions were unknown. During the two decades preceding our entrance into the World War, the economy had expanded rapidly but without serious interruption. The liquidation of 1920-21 was severe—estimates placed the number of unemployed as high as five million—but the speedy recovery reduced the devastation to a minimum. The seven good years that followed 1922 made optimists of us all. Never was change more rapid and never were the results more beneficial. While economists analyzed the marvelous mechanism of economic balance, the population sang hymns of praise to the New Era.[2]

The analyses were scarcely completed and the hymns were still echoing when the long period of economic expansion came to an abrupt halt. As the contraction gained momentum, the optimism engendered by the prosperity of the past was gradually obliterated. No longer could one blithely maintain that a competitive system held wastes to a minimum; no longer could one be certain that a renewed expansion was inevitable. As industry after industry was unable to earn a profit, and as the number of unemployed was augmented by millions, economic stability became a remembrance of things past.

Just as the remembrance was itself fading, the economy began to revive under the protection of President Roosevelt. With the passage of time, the recovery was accelerated and belief in economic stability was rehabilitated. But the expansion petered out, and a contraction of unparalleled rapidity set in. When hope of self-correction faded, President Roosevelt proposed new measures to ensure by legislation that which could not be secured by competition. The stabilization of the economy remained the *summum bonum* of the New Deal.

Potent alike in the past and in the present, the ideal of economic stability does not easily permit of unequivocal definition. Clearly, it has never meant, nor does it now mean, that economic change should be arrested. If the simple-minded be disregarded and the philosophers be ignored, the ideal of economic stability permits of reasonable interpretation: namely, the full and efficient utilization of available human and material resources.

These criteria must be loosely applied. Not the total adult population, but the total number of laborers customarily attached to industry, establishes the norm of maximum employment; not engineering estimates, but existing plant and equipment of standard quality, suggest the measure of capacity. Efficiency implies that similar resources earn approximately similar returns. When Soviet Russia forces Kulaks to fish in northern waters and pays them a bare subsistence wage, when Germany conscripts the unemployed to drain the marshes of East Prussia and recompenses them with a mark a day and keep, one may be justified in talking of the full utilization but surely not of the efficient utilization of available resources.[3]

The major tradition in economics was so greatly preoccupied with analyzing the forces determining the distribution of the annual income that it paid slight attention to the production of the income. Implicit was the assumption that all resources were fully employed. Not that the periodic underemployment of men and machines

213

completely escaped attention. Karl Marx was, of course, greatly concerned with the problem, and at the turn of the century more moderate dissenters were attracted to the study of business cycles. However, the expansive powers of the economy were so great, especially in the United States, that the majority of students took little interest in the underutilization of resources. Business contractions were few and far between; hence they could well be considered minor variations on a major theme.[4]

When one recalls that between the Civil War and the World War the expansion of the economy was subjected to only two major interruptions, one can well appreciate why economists considered depressions a minor matter. Moreover, the period after 1914 reinforced the optimistic bias; except for the readjustment incidental to shifting from a war to a peace basis, the economy prospered. The belief in economic stability—the cornerstone of the New Era—appeared reasonable. The events after 1929 proved, however, that the belief was founded more on fancy than on fact. Despite its dénouement during the depression, the belief in economic stability survived. The New Deal was largely created in its image and the Recovery Message of April, 1938, was written under its spell. A belief so potent should not escape analysis.

Although economists have seen fit to ignore or minimize its importance, technology is the true master of the modern world. Even the organized power of Indian religion is unable to halt the advance of Lancashire machinery. Not only is technology largely in control of the long-time trend, but it plays an important role in conditioning economic fluctuations of shorter duration. In the first instance, new industries depend upon technological progress, and new industries have always left their impress upon cycles of economic expansion. During the period of gestation a new industry "is likely to oscillate between no production at all and a nominal volume of output," but once the manufacturing and marketing hurdles have been overcome, the rate of growth is likely to be extremely rapid.[5]

From the end of tl : Civil War until the close of the century, the expansioı of the railroad industry was of the greatest importance ir determining the course of the economy. As many miles f track were laid in the five-year period from 1868 to 1873, as in the thirty years preceding the outbreak of the war. Moreover, the revival in railroad building contributed greatly to the recovery of the late seventies and guided the fortunes of the economy until the depression of the nineties. Between the turn of the century and the outbreak of the World War, the electrical industry forged to the front. The production of kilowatt hours increased in the decade from 1902 to 1912 no less than fourfold, and the total mileage of electric railways increased threefold.[6]

Less obvious but perhaps of even greater importance was the doubling of the population between 1870 and 1900. From a base of 38 million in 1870, there occurred a regular decennial increase of approximately 12 million; at the turn of the century, the population totaled 76 million. The gain between 1900 and 1910 was even greater, for this decade witnessed an increase of approximately 16 million. Not less than 40 per cent of the total increase of 50 million between 1870 and 1910 could be accounted for by immigration. Although the detailed figures are unavailable, there can be no doubt whatever that this phenomenal increase in population must have been associated with phenomenal activity in residential, commercial, and industrial construction.[7]

To concentrate upon the trio—population, construction, and railroads—in sketching the period between the Civil War and the World War doubtless leads to the neglect of important variables; but the basic pattern is probably correct. During the nineteen twenties, the props of the economy were construction and the automobile.

Important for the student of economic stabilization is the incontrovertible fact that retardation in the rate of growth is typical of all industries. This observation gains in significance when one recalls that the articulation of the modern economy facilitates the transference of stimuli. Acceleration, retardation, and decline are never isolated; their influence always transcends the boundaries of a single industry.

For instance, at the beginning of the twenties, a large building boom got under way, precipitated by shortages brought on by the low level of wartime construction and enhanced by additions to, and redistribution in, our population. Before many months had elapsed, the railroad, steel, lumber, cement, copper, and a host of other industries felt the stimulus. The mutual dependence of industrial expansion on rising incomes and of rising incomes on industrial expansion ensured a boom of considerable magnitude. Activity in residential construction was concentrated on providing dwellings for the lower and upper middle class: small houses were sold or mortgaged to the former; apartment houses and hotels were erected for the latter. By 1928, the market appeared amply exploited. Since private capital has always shied clear of building for the poor—the risks are too great and the returns too small—residential construction began to peter out.[8]

Automobiles tell a similar story. Although the industry was able to expand rapidly in the years immediately preceding and following the World War, the depression of 1920-21 found it in serious straits. The wealthy were supplied with vehicles and those in moderate circumstances were unable to purchase, above all were unable to finance, such a sizable investment. Technological improvements reduced the costs of manufacturing, and installment credit proved a great marketing boon. The expansion was renewed and, in turn, it stimulated the rubber, petroleum, steel, glass, lumber, and many other industries. Between 1918 and 1922, registration figures increased from 6 to 12 million and during the next four years they mounted to 22 million. Conspicuous consumption might prove a further stimulus but clearly the rate of growth could not be maintained. Since the poor could purchase used cars at a price that new units could not hope to approximate, a marked retardation in the rate of expansion was inevitable.[9]

Just as rapid advances in the construction and the automobile industries swelled the national income, the retardation in their rate of growth was certain to depress the economy. The automobile had been especially stimulating, for it conditioned the growth of suburbs, the radical alterations in distribution, and the diversification of recreation. Above all, the road system was vastly enlarged and improved. As the number of automobiles grew more slowly, repair work would in part take the place of new construction. In many sections of the economy, additional capacity would be less urgent; replacement of existing capacity would suffice.

Only the emergence of new industries, or the more rapid growth of old industries, could have prevented the decline in general economic activity that retardation in the rate of growth of construction and automobiles was certain to engender. The latter twenties did witness a marked expansion in the radio and electrical-appliance industries, but these could not fill the gap. It must not be overlooked that the combined value of output of the construction and automobile industries in 1928 exceeded 10 billion dollars, while radio was not even in the billion-dollar class.[10]

The experience of the United States after the collapse of the New Era illustrates even more clearly than does the New Era itself the instabilities that result from marked variations in the growth of important industries. Residential construction totaled almost 3 billion dollars in 1928, but in 1932 the figure was less than 300 million; commercial and factory construction declined at a parallel rate, from 1,400 million dollars in 1928 to 165 million dollars in 1932. Automobile production likewise plummeted from a record of more than 5½ million cars in 1929 to one of less than 1½ million in 1932. These reductions were, of course, reflected in the production of allied industries. Early in 1933, the output of the iron and steel industry totaled but 24 per cent, that of the cement industry but 18 per cent, of their July, 1929, production.[11]

Allies during the New Era and the Depression, the automobile and construction industries parted ways shortly before the beginning of the New Deal. So strong was the replacement demand for automobiles that the industry was able to expand in midsummer of 1932, an expansion that became considerably broader after the inauguration of President Roosevelt. Although less than 1½ million cars were produced in 1932, more than 4½ million were turned out in 1936. Not until the latter part of 1937 was the progress of the automobile industry arrested. During the New Deal, construction made, however, only a modest comeback, and even this revival largely reflected governmental spendings for public works. The inability of the Roosevelt recovery to maintain itself can, in the first instance, be explained by the failure of construction to revive.[12]

Another contribution of technology to the instability of modern economies results from the fact that the enlargement of the means of production is greatly affected by the acceleration in the demand for finished products. Although the output of manufactured consumption goods declined only 20 per cent between 1929 and 1933, the production of the capital-goods industries dropped no less than 80 per cent. During the twenties, the equipment industries were rapidly expanded to enable the consumption-goods industries to meet the rising demand for their products. Since a reduction in the rate of increase for consumers' goods would have cut the output of capital goods, a decrease of 20 per cent could not fail to raise havoc. Unfortunately, "no magic of institutional formulae can make these two rates equal."[13]

To eradicate completely the technological precipitant of economic fluctuations would necessitate controlling the rate of growth of new industries as well as modifying the relations now existing between the capital-goods and consumption-goods industries. At present, entrepreneurs can secure capital whenever their prospective activities promise sizable profits. To control the growth of new industries implies, therefore, radical changes in the capital market, changes that look forward to the specific allocation of new funds. The experience of the World War, the more recent history of Soviet Russia, Italy, and Germany, the contemporary rearmament programs of England and France disclose that the control over new investment is inextricably bound up with autocratic political power. Despite the rantings of conservatives, such power is nonexistent in the United States.

Absence of radical changes in our prevailing institutions does not preclude, however, partial controls over technological forces. For several decades, the state has assumed an ever larger role as the guardian of quasi-public corporations and as the director of public enterprises. Instabilities attendant upon the differential rates of growth of important industries in the private economy might long be tolerated because of the high price of control. Yet a more direct and coordinated supervision over the size and timing of capital expenditures of railroads and other public utilities—sectors that are today under the substantial control of the state—might go far to compensate for fluctuations produced by the private economy.

More important, however, is the enlargement of the state's direct entrepreneurial activity. During these past years, the public's approach to federal financing has undergone marked changes; unfortunately, the banking community has lagged far behind. But as the fears about a mounting public debt begin to recede, and more attention is devoted to the social contributions of public improvements, the government will have a greatly widened field for therapeutic effort. If the private economy cannot utilize to the full the available resources of men and materials, the public economy must be conditioned to take up the slack. Clearly, the problems of adjustment are difficult, but only a cynic would dare to prejudge the results. Technology may long continue to engender substantial fluctuations in the economy, but curative, if not preventative measures, appear on the horizon.

If technology is at the root of modern economic instability, it receives yeoman assistance from psychology. Subject to constant change, economic data are difficult to interpret. Since all interpretations are influenced by the preconceptions of the interpreter, the genesis and growth of these preconceptions are crucial. Projection is the key mechanism, for past experience is the only guide to future action.

Despite the phenomenal alteration in the American economy between the Civil War and the World War, the major outlines are clear. Although the depressions of the seventies and the nineties brought a halt to the expansional development, they were unable to deflect the trend for long. Nor could the minor reversals succeed where the major ones had failed. Based upon the most solid foundation of expansions in physical production and employment, a strong tradition of business optimism was generated, a tradition that became increasingly entrenched as the nineties were left behind.

During the postwar liquidation of 1920-21, the economy was rudely shaken. The collapse was severe, but the fact that it had been more or less expected—a readjustment from a war to a peace basis could not be painless—modified its evil consequences. Scholastics have attempted to dehumanize economics, but there is no reason to doubt that the market place reacts strongly to the emotions of traders. So strong was the optimistic bias of American business that, once the most intense manifestations of the liquidation had spent themselves, new investment was undertaken. The construction and automobile industries did not fear the future, and as they revived the entire economy responded.[14]

As farms were turned into suburbs and suburbs were turned into cities, the optimism of the public grew substantially, for increases in physical production were the prelude to increases in profits. Just as the growth of one industry could not fail to stimulate other industries, so optimism spread through the land. Although the manufacturer of automobile parts might have doubted the wisdom of selling an automobile to a laborer whose weekly income did not exceed 40 dollars; although the manufacturer of building materials might not have viewed with favor the sale of a house to a clerk whose annual income totaled 2,500 dollars—these doubts were easily dissipated by larger orders and still larger profits.

As increasing numbers of the business community viewed the future optimistically, the future had increasing possibility of justifying their optimism. Favorable evaluations led to new investments and new investments increased the stream of purchasing power, a development that justified the favorable evaluations. Demand was supply and supply was demand. Although the tables and graphs of statisticians could be appreciated only after study, the millions of new houses and the tens of millions of new automobiles were beyond dispute. If opportunities for investment exist—and the American economy had an excellent record of such opportunities—expansion awaits upon a favorable evaluation of the future. In the twenties, automobiles and construction appeared promising; a strong optimism did the rest. The New Era was no historical sport; it followed a conventional pattern.

Sentiments are infectious. Eras of religious frenzy share the stage with eras of speculative frenzy. The nineteen twenties were vulnerable to speculation: tradition favored optimism; the facts favored optimism; it is hardly surprising that optimism came and conquered. Special interests left few stones unturned to heighten the mood, a process that cheap printing and cheap speaking greatly facilitated. The advantages of investing in stocks and real estate were related to the blind by ear and to the deaf by eye; the public at large was bombarded by brochure and broadcast.*[15]

It was, however, more or less inevitable that the prevailing optimism should eventually overshoot the mark. The rapid expansion of the economy could more easily be admired than analyzed. It was not easy to estimate correctly the retardation in the rate of growth of the construction and automobile industries; but if allowance were not made for retardation, the future could not fail to prove the expectations wrong. Construction began to decline in 1928, and automobiles ran into trouble at the turn of the year; by July, 1929, the majority of indices had reached their height. The collapse of the stock market in October was a belated recognition of incorrect evaluations. If business failed to advance, if, worse still, it actually declined, stock-market prices were clearly in need of radical revision. And business gave every evidence of slackening, if not of declining.

Throughout the New Era, the technological and psychological factors were mutually stimulating. So, too, on the decline. The severe reduction in the prices of equities during the last months of 1929—a reduction that cut the value of shares on the New York Stock Exchange from approximately 100 to 65 billion dollars—although a re-

* During the serious depression that preceded Hitler's assumption of office, a Prussian bureaucrat of Socialist persuasion sought to increase the consumption of electricity. To this end he secured, at sacrifice prices, large numbers of old radios which he distributed freely among the farm population. In addition to the current used for radios, it was anticipated that farmers would no longer go to bed at sundown and the load factor for lighting would therefore increase substantially. The plan was a great success, in fact, so great that Hitler was able to carry his message into every hamlet.

flection of past declines in business activity, could not fail to hasten future declines. New investment was held in abeyance and even new consumption was stayed in its tracks. As many awakened to the fact that their wealth was not only intangible but also ephemeral, the demand for country estates and expensive automobiles dropped swiftly.

The tradition of business optimism was, however, so firmly entrenched that even the disastrous decline in stock-market prices was viewed calmly. The reiteration of President Hoover that the economy was fundamentally stable, and his promise that the decline in business activity would be short-lived, was more than political propaganda. This conviction was not restricted to party lines but rather reflected general sentiment. In view of the ingrained optimism, it is small wonder that every bend in the statistical indicators was hailed as the turning point. Not until midsummer of 1931 was faith abandoned. Thereafter pessimism swept the land, feeding on itself in much the same way as had the optimism of the New Era. Though new capital issues totaled in excess of 10 billion dollars in 1929 they dropped to 3 billion dollars in 1931 and, in 1932, they did not exceed one billion.

Since the existing level of business activity left unutilized a large percentage of available capacity, the disinclination to invest was well founded. But the reluctance to expand also reflected a pessimistic attitude about the future level of activity, which itself depended in large measure upon the rate of new investment. If optimism led to mania, pessimism led to panic. Liquidity became the new fetish. The constant decline in prevailing prices precipitated the turning of assets into cash, a process that led to the further reduction of prices. As the banking crisis of March, 1933, so clearly illustrated, the mad scramble for liquidity brought the economy very close to self-liquidation.[16]

President Roosevelt's dictum that we have nothing to fear but fear was not only excellent prose but excellent economics. The policy of watchful waiting followed by President Hoover was not foolish, for it assumed that time would create expansive factors. It underestimated, however, the disruptive influences of cumulative liquidation. Pessimism was not only impeding new investment, but it was also successfully destroying the old. As President Roosevelt so clearly perceived, economic recovery hinged upon a fundamental change in prevailing attitudes.

Responsive to the strenuous efforts that the federal government made to strengthen the underpinnings of the economy, business opinion improved as soon as the New Deal got under way. The inventory boom of the spring and summer was proof of the successful change in mood. Of course, success had its price. Much of the new legislation interfered so radically with the preconceptions of industrialists that the stimulation was either partially or completely dissipated. Fiscal policy was probably most upsetting. But production and employment grew apace and the national income commenced to retrace slowly the ground that it had lost during the blistering depression. However, the expansion of the economy did not lead to rampant optimism; in fact, it hardly led to optimism at all. The shock of the preceding years had been so intense that many months had to pass before confidence in the future was again restored. Moreover, radical departures in public policy could not fail to unsettle the timid whose nerves had been badly shattered by the debacle.

Trends were projected with great care; the moral of the depression was not lost with the first increase in business activity. Lagging investments, typical of the first three years of President Roosevelt's administration, but atypical of the twenties, illustrated the new conservatism in business expectations. The uncertainty that attached to the changing role of the state in economic life was doubtless a major deterrent, but the absence of good opportunities for speculative investments was probably more potent.

Though the relations between government and business did not improve during 1936 and 1937, the output of durable producers' goods rose markedly. If the depression had faded more quickly, or if the hostility toward the administration had been absent, the expansion might well have been more intense. The dead hand of the past was, however, powerful during the unparalleled decline that set in toward the end of 1937; public pressure could not, as in 1929, prevent private enterprise from adopting extremely cautious policies.

Industrial capitalism attests the achievements of enterprising individuals who in a search for power demolished the homes of their fathers and twisted the souls of their children. Individual initiative can hardly be overestimated. But it must not be forgotten that in the modern market the most powerful individual is severely limited by the mass. Since the level of business activity is intimately dependent upon the expectations of the business community, and since the immediate future is so directly determined by these expectations, nobody can afford to disregard the mass. One must swim with the tide and the exceptional man is he who knows when the tide is about to turn.

Under pressure to estimate the future, the business community carefully evaluates the past, not the far-distant but the more recent past, for in a changing economy, the data of old blur rapidly and are subject to accelerated obsolescence. At the turn of the century, output of bituminous coal may well have been an important index, but the development of water power, fuel oil, and natural gas have forced it into the background. Cumulative changes are greatly dependent upon the projection of present conditions. If prosperity breeds a belief in further expansion, new investment will be enhanced and the expansion will thereby be ensured. If contraction precipitates a feeling of uncertainty about the future, liquidation of assets will proceed apace, and unemployment and bankruptcies will mount.

Truth and error are statistical concepts. In a world gone mad, insanity is no disease. During the twenties, an occasional banker might have doubted the wisdom of lending to South American countries, recognizing that the annihilation of political opponents was at best an uncertain investment. Yet as long as debtors were able to service their loans, and as long as a segment of the invest-

228

ment community was willing to take a chance, only the most powerful banker could withstand the pressure. Although expensive apartment houses were being erected at a very rapid rate toward the end of the New Era, entrepreneurs of still more and more expensive ones, whose plans indicated reasonable prospects of returns, could not be denied funds. One can afford to go against the trend only when the trend is about to turn. To assess the future of the economy, it is necessary to assess the attitudes of the business community, making due allowance for the fact that irrational attitudes frequently justify themselves.

Expectations can, however, be proved false. Failure to discount the weakening of expansionary stimuli is the most frequent cause of error. If approaching retardation in the rate of growth of the automobile industry had been appreciated toward the end of the New Era, reduced investments in expensive housing would have been advisable. Moreover, if retardation in the rate of growth of new construction had been perceived, new additions to automobile plant and equipment could have been kept at a more modest figure.

Faith in economic stability is little strengthened by a review of the psychological determinants of business expectations. Business suffers from an optimistic bias and painless policies make powerful politicians. Yet partial controls to limit the scope of cumulative reactions should not prove impossible. In the past, the government has frequently contributed to intensifying rather than to moderating the dominant mood. During the New Era, the Federal Reserve System kept money rates low and the

Department of State encouraged foreign lending; during the New Deal, the banking community was not educated to view deficit financing favorably and the struggle with public utilities was not compromised. As politicians grow in wisdom and as civil servants grow in independence, the government will be able to contribute greatly to correcting the exaggerated reactions of the business community to future prospects. In addition, as business itself becomes increasingly conscious that, wherever possible, the most enlightened policy is to maximize profits not in the immediate future but rather over a span of years, more moderation can be anticipated. Finally, the varied experience of the economy since the World War makes a repetition of the New Era's uncontrolled optimism as improbable as a repetition of the Great Depression's uncontrolled pessimism. To eliminate the psychological causes of economic instability is hopeless; to moderate them is conceivable.

For centuries, the Western World has been greatly influenced by the ethics of Protestantism, which ascribe great importance to work and foresight. Though they were much influenced by the Old Testament, both Luther and Calvin, especially Calvin, overlooked the Wisdom Books which emphasized the sterility of accumulation and affirmed the fertility of expenditure. As industrial capitalism expanded, the bourgeoisie of England and the United States admired ever more highly the twin virtues of effort and abstinence. Emphasis was placed upon men of spirit who transformed themselves into men of capital, though silence was maintained about the fact that most transformations occurred in the womb. Wealth has always been more easy to inherit than to acquire. During the nineteenth century, many succeeded, however, in ending their days amidst a plenty unknown to them in their youth, thereby offering inductive verification of the code. In this milieu, labor and savings were viewed as the foundations of wealth. That artificial increases in bank deposits might materially influence the structure of production, and that such influence need not necessarily be injurious, was a doctrine so repugnant that it did not warrant consideration. Morals impeded analysis. The World War, however, stripped the veil from the moralists, for monetary manipulations proved most useful. Money was readmitted to economic analysis, and in a flush of enthusiasm, that has not yet died down, it was assumed that the behavior of money could explain all, and its control cure all.[17]

Possessed of the power to create and destroy deposits, banks have made increasing use of the privilege. Total deposits of all American banks totaled about 18,500 million dollars at the outbreak of the World War, whence they increased more than 100 per cent until brought to a halt by the liquidation of 1920-21. After decreasing by several billions, they rose rapidly as the economy renewed its expansion. By the end of the New Era they totaled 55 billion. The long and severe depression reduced them radically; in June, 1933, they approximated 38 billion dollars. Once again, they increased rapidly; and four years after the banking crisis, they totaled about 51 billion, a gain of more than 35 per cent.[18]

The magnitude of these changes suggests that economists can ill afford to disregard the banking mechanism, no matter how greatly they differ in their evaluation of the present role of money. These striking fluctuations in bank deposits were in the first instance a reflection of changes in bank assets, which in turn were closely related to alterations in general business conditions. Certain doctors are convinced that changes in bank deposits bring about changes in business, while certain other doctors are equally convinced that changes in business bring about changes in bank deposits. A few doctors believe that both contentions are extreme, and surmise that the truth lies between.

Although it has been gospel for many generations that capital is formed by savings, this dogma is simple but not pure. Banks can create capital. If the economy possesses unused resources of men and materials, the process of capital formation with the aid of the banks is extremely efficacious. If bank deposits could not be expanded, increases in the production of capital goods would have to wait upon decreases in the production of consumption goods. But a reduction in the latter would demolish any interest in expanding the former.[19]

In reviewing the New Era, one is impressed with the fact that its prosperity was enhanced—but not caused —by the expansion in the money supply. If bank deposits had not been enlarged, an expansion in general business might well have taken place, but it would probably have been considerably more moderate. If all new investment had been forced to depend upon real savings, the rate of capital accumulation would have been vastly slower. Moreover, additions to the money supply stimulated speculation in real estate and securities. While the prices of equities were on the rise, business sentiment became increasingly optimistic, a factor of no small importance in furthering the general expansion.

The gain was, of course, short-lived. Once business began to contract, the behavior of money proved as depressing as it had previously proved stimulating. With the collapse of the stock market, business expectations underwent a marked turn for the worse, which reduced the willingness of bankers to lend and of investors to borrow. As old loans were called and new loans were refused, bank deposits declined. This process led to accelerated declines in business activity. As the demand for men and materials weakened, prices fell and profits disappeared. By 1931, the cumulative process was well under way and the half-hearted attempts of the government to expand the money supply were woefully inadequate.

By the end of 1932, total bank deposits had declined 15 billion dollars or more than 25 per cent from their New Era high, and the banking crisis that welcomed President Roosevelt into office was not solved without liquidating an additional 2 billion dollars of deposits. Although forces working toward the expansion of business were present at the beginning of 1933, the further weakening of an already weak banking structure could not fail to have bad results. The new administration, however, took drastic steps to counteract the contraction of deposits. Appropriations for direct relief were partially responsible for an increase in bank deposits, and other recovery measures stimulated further increases. December, 1934, found deposits at a figure 7 billion greater than June, 1933; and by December, 1935, they had increased 11 billion, a total rise of 30 per cent in less than three years. Large-scale spending, financed through the sale of government bonds to the banks, was almost solely responsible for the increases in deposits. Between June, 1933, and December, 1935, all member banks enlarged their holdings of direct and fully guaranteed governmental bonds by 5,400 million dollars, while during this same period their loans decreased 700 million dollars.[20]

Total deposits continued to mount rapidly until they reached a high of almost 54 billion dollars in December, 1936, an advance during the New Deal of 16 billion, or more than 40 per cent. Although loans continued to increase thereafter, investments declined, in largest measure a reflection of reduced holdings of government bonds.[21]

The New Deal bears striking similarity, yet stands in striking contrast, to the New Era. In both periods, bank deposits increased, though the acceleration was more marked in the latter. So much for the similarity; more important is the contrast. During the twenties, increased loans and investments, a reflection of the increasing optimism of bankers about the future trend of business, were responsible for the expansion in the money supply. Bank portfolios contained an increasing number of loans and investments in real estate and securities. The rapid rise of bank deposits during the New Deal must largely be interpreted in terms of federal deficit financing through the banking system; increased investments in government bonds predominate.

The collapse of the New Era showed that price fluctuations in the assets of the private economy can be so intense as to precipitate declines in business activity and bank deposits. But one need be no Cassandra to view with concern, if not with alarm, the expansion of bank deposits backed by public assets. Clearly, increases based on governmental deficits cannot continue indefinitely; clearly, the values of government bonds may likewise fluctuate. A decline of 10 per cent in the price of government bonds would place the banking system in a precarious position.

The review of the postwar developments has disclosed frequent and large changes in the money supply. Controlled largely by the demands of entrepreneurs and the government, influenced greatly by the anticipations of bankers about the future trend of business activity, fluctuations in the money supply can themselves affect the activity and anticipations of business.

For many decades, political control over banking has been growing apace; in fact, the most ardent admirers of laissez-faire were never convinced that competition in the money market was more blessing than curse. At the outbreak of the World War, the Bank of England was supreme not only in London but wherever British trade predominated, and the recent establishment of the Federal Reserve System had opened the way for strong centralized controls in the United States. Four years of hostilities catapulted the central banks of all belligerents into a position of dominance from which the armistice was unable to dislodge them. Only in the United States were centralized controls over banking substantially reduced. But the severe depression that followed the collapse of the New Era helped to reestablish the power, if not the prestige, of the Federal Reserve System.

The heavy toll taken by the periodic liquidation of large quantities of bank deposits has led several students to propose reforms aimed at divorcing the money supply from bank assets. Clearly, to remove "the reciprocally aggravating effects which are characteristic of the present relations between business activity and the stock of money" would prove desirable. The fugitive literature has called attention to striking technical difficulties, and the political opposition of the banking community can hardly be overestimated. Crucial, however, is the probability that changes in velocity and the use of money substitutes will continue to permit business to intensify its optimistic and pessimistic moods.[22]

The recent experience of England, Sweden, and the United States leads one to search for more moderate, but also more feasible controls. Governmental intervention can assuredly help to stem an untoward contraction in bank deposits, just as it can prevent a runaway expansion. The limits of successful central banking policy are unknown, but the last years have proved that state action can contribute greatly to increasing the stability of the money supply. Complete success will probably never be possible, but continued experimentation promises much.

Although the prewar economy established a presumption in favor of the belief in economic stability, a belief that the New Era surely strengthened, economic developments since 1929 have proved discomforting. Itself a testimonial to economic instability, the last decade has afforded us an opportunity to revise our evaluation of the stable twenties. Cumulative interactions of technological, psychological, and monetary forces have kept the postwar economy in constant turmoil. Differential rates of growth of important industries, and exaggerated reactions of the capital-goods industries to changes in the demand for consumers' goods, have laid the foundation for substantial fluctuations. Since the business community usually estimates the future by projecting the present, prevailing trends are intensified. Finally, a banking system possessed of the power to increase and decrease the money supply by 30 or 40 per cent within a three-year period cannot fail to stimulate fluctuations already under way, and can, upon occasion, actually generate such fluctuations.[23] Only as these factors are brought under control can economic stability be transformed from a pious wish into a solid fact.

But further difficulties would have to be met. Since the adjustment among the myriad pieces of the economy depends upon the price mechanism, and since the price mechanism suffers from serious imperfections, the underutilization and the inefficient utilization of available resources would remain to mock.

In the past as in the present, the price mechanism has been manipulated. Individual or collective control over supply has been frequent, if not typical. Enlarged investments in plant and equipment have increased the incentives of industry to cooperate. Failure to place limits upon competitive behavior ensured that, under conditions of excess capacity, prices would be driven to a point so low that no firm could earn a profit. The history of the steel, cement, gasoline, and copper industries—to mention only outstanding examples—illustrates the efforts currently devoted to controlling price competition. Nor is this surprising, for "to insist that producers shall compete unchecked appears to amount to inviting competition, and private enterprise with it, to commit suicide."[24]

Although the law of the land prohibits agreements among competitors on prices and production, a review of the available evidence—one must not forget that there is a premium on silence, for heavy fines and a jail sentence await the guilty—permits of little doubt that tacit understandings are almost as efficacious as legal agreements. It must not be overlooked, however, that in a changing economy failure to play ball is upon occasion more lucrative than cooperation. Pressure to agree on prices cannot be denied, but one must not forget that large premiums await the successful innovator—in colloquial language, the chiseler.[25]

Price control by producers finds its counterpart in wage control by unions. To recall that 60 per cent of the national income is more or less regularly paid out in wages and salaries illustrates the importance of these controls. Before the World War, strong unions were limited "to transportation, building, printing and local mining industries. During the War and first post-war prosperity unionism spread to the clothing and metal trades but proved only temporary in the latter." In 1930, only 10 per cent of all nonagricultural employees were members of trade unions. Since limitation of the supply of labor is crucial for effective control over price, the growth of unionism was facilitated by the immobility of certain industries—building, transportation, mining. Clothing is the exception which permits of explanation in terms of "skill and militancy of leadership and public interest and concern . . . with the sweatshop."[26]

The poor statistical showing of union membership doubtless leads to underestimating the true influence of labor organization on the determination of wages. To sabotage the growth of unionism, employers have long used the weapon of meeting, and frequently exceeding, union wages. The frequent relocation of industry has also proved a successful method of escaping union pressure. The large expansion in union membership during the New Deal, and the increasing social and legal limitations upon entrepreneurial escape from union standards, have substantially increased the control of unions over the supply and price of labor.

Restraints exercised by manufacturers and unions do not exhaust the story of price controls. In 1934, agriculture, public utilities, and the government accounted for 19 billion dollars out of a total gross national product of 56 billion dollars. In these three sectors, prices are today as much under the control of the law as they are under the control of the market. If finance be added to the regulated section, an addition easily justified in light of the dominance of the government in banking, almost 50 per cent of the national product is directly affected by price controls.[27]

Under conditions of perfect mobility of the factors of production, one can anticipate the full utilization of available resources, an anticipation unwarranted if perfect mobility does not exist. The contemporary world abounds in illustrations of unused capacity coexisting with prices above variable costs, just as substantial unemployment impairs but slightly the wage rates of the employed. Nor are these anomalies difficult to explain. Powerful concerns can ill afford to reduce their prices and heighten the risk of insolvency on the theory that if all prices were reduced the solvency of the economy could more easily be assured. Likewise, the existence of specific wages so high as to hinder new investment does not imply that strong unions should offer wage reductions. The losses from such reductions are obvious; the gains are highly uncertain. There can be no doubt that imperfections in the pricing mechanism contribute to the underutilization of available resources. Unless price controls can be eliminated, economic stabilization must remain unrealized.

Moreover, price controls insure not only underutilization, but also faulty allocation, of available resources. Despite the fact that additional capital could earn a larger return elsewhere, powerful controls might force its investment in protected sectors. The same holds true of the labor market. The exclusion policy of strong unions forces workers to flood certain industries. Willing to accept three dollars per day on a Detroit assembly line, the

Southern yokel must sell himself to a Mississippi planter for three dollars a week.

Despite this formidable evidence, it is not certain that the last decades have witnessed an intensification of price controls. No doubt, the pattern of competition has been constantly modified, yet this modification is proof neither of the reduction nor the elimination of competition. Improvements in transportation and communication have contributed so markedly to the destruction of local monopolies that the fluidity of the modern market may well equal, if it does not exceed, that which formerly prevailed. Irrespective of the trend, the search for economic stability must be evaluated in terms of sustained imperfections in the price mechanism. In agriculture, producers' control over supply and price has been absent, but new investment has not been guided solely by pecuniary calculation; in industry, the search for money profits has been so intense that industrialists, determined to control market price, have not hesitated to flout common and statutory law.[28]

In the writings of the orthodox economists, the problems connected with the full and efficient utilization of available resources were not analyzed. The optimum was simply assumed. Karl Marx protested but in vain, for the exhortations of pariahs are never taken seriously. Moreover, Marx's prophecies went awry. Although the danger of the strong growing stronger and the weak growing weaker was real, Marx overestimated the advantages of large-scale enterprise. Costs cannot fall indefinitely and increasing size breeds inflexibility. The eventual unleashing of corrective influence does not, however, absolve the price mechanism of serious shortcomings.

Conscious that corporations, trade unions, and governmental commissions exercise substantial controls over production and prices, many students, including the skeptical Mr. Roosevelt, believe that salvation lies in the reestablishment of that which never existed. Despite the many pretty pictures of perfect markets that fill the pages of classical economics, there is no historical evidence to prove the existence of perfect competition. Assuredly, contemporary prices do not follow the patterns found in the economics of old, but the important question is whether they follow the patterns of the economies of old.

The action of strong blocs—corporate, labor, and agricultural—to control the market in the hope of bettering their economic position places additional difficulties in the path of securing a stable economy in which resources are fully and efficiently employed. In fact, those who seek to ensure a market uncontrolled either by the state or by powerful interests in the state, must be theoreticians rather than historians. Competition implies proximate equality of bargaining power, a condition unknown during five thousand years of recorded history. Differentials in power were the basis of Plato's Republic just as they are typical of Stalin's Russia.

But if no system has been devised to prevent the exploitation of one group by another, it does not follow that all systems are equally exploitative. Clearly, the imperfectly competitive system of industrial capitalism makes a more adequate and more efficient use of available economic resources than does the caste system of India. Despite the fact that technology proscribed the erection of thousands of steel mills and tradition prescribed the widest scope for individual initiative, a lethargic electorate and a biased judiciary succeeded during the last century in correcting the worse abuses of economic power. In recent years, the checks have become vastly greater. Although democracy is typified by division of power and is propelled by compromise, it has not been impotent in dealing with economic oligarchy.

The struggle of powerful groups to control the price mechanism will doubtless continue, and only a rampant optimist will fail to discount the influence of these struggles upon the achievement of economic stability. The goal may never be reached but progress toward the goal is not impossible. In the past, political techniques have proved moderately efficient in correcting the worst excrescences of economic competition, and there is no reason to doubt that the future will witness marked extensions of these controls.

The economic fluctuations of the last decades can largely be explained by the interaction of technological, psychological, and monetary factors, though the fluctuations were intensified by imperfections of the pricing mechanism. Unless these several factors are subject to control, economic stability must remain an illusion. Since complete control appears neither imminent nor potential, belief in economic stability must be scrapped. Yet cynicism need not replace faith. Partial controls can accomplish much. Technological progress and speculative investments will probably continue in the future, as they have in the past, to precipitate periods of substantial expansion. A more careful application of existing controls, and an enterprising search for new controls, can contribute greatly to moderating the advances and to checking the retreats. But this modest expectation may well be extreme.

Although much of life is spent working to eat and eating to work, man does not live only in the market or only for the market. In a world divided not only into those who have and those who have not, but also into those who believe and those who do not believe, warfare between men is firmly established. Given a bone and a mate, the most belligerent of the animal kingdom becomes docile. Man alone is an exception; he needs more. Unless his creations find acceptance, unless they are at least respected, his latent hostility becomes overt. Since life itself leads to differentiation, the causes for friction multiply. Nor must it be forgotten that defeat in battle means destruction at home. Jehovah's victory over Baal was accompanied by the rape of women who prayed to Baal and the slaughter of men who trusted in Baal.

For thousands of years men have striven to obtain in war what they could not secure peacefully. Most of the struggles have been in vain, for victory in battle is frequently Pyrrhic. Since envy is stronger than reason and vitality is seldom compatible with wisdom, the struggles continue. Erased from memory is the fact that Alexander succumbed to a germ and Napoleon was vanquished by the snow.

Soldiers drill, for tomorrow they march. Cannon must answer cannon. Increasingly the resources and labor of every country are conscripted for military purposes. Increasingly, dictatorships and democracies differ only in the means of conscription. Increasingly, all criteria of economic efficiency save one—military preparedness—are being scuttled. In many lands, naïve youngsters approve enthusiastically; in others, mature men act with serious deliberation; in still others, the public is just beginning to comprehend. The race gains momentum; the costs begin to mount; opposition is limited to a sigh of regret. Fear is master; no one denies him tribute. Gold does not suffice; even dreams must be sacrificed. On the altar of political expediency, the illusion of economic stability is finally consumed. "For in the multitude of dreams and many words are also divers vanities." But Ecclesiastes further reminds us that "wisdom is a defense, and money is a defense: but the excellency of knowledge is, that wisdom giveth life to them that have it."

APPENDIXES

APPENDIX I

INSTALLMENT SELLING

Seeking to explain the prolonged prosperity of the twenties, many observers stumbled upon installment selling. A Puritan community could not easily reconcile itself to the belief that the private vice of going into debt was certain to be a public benefit. In the past, such action had always been viewed askance but modern businessmen argued that it was a boon, both to the individual consumer and to the economy at large. In order to overcome the antagonism of conservatives, the automobile industry, which was greatly dependent upon the use of installment selling, facilitated the publication of the first detailed study of consumer credit. Nothing is so destructive to dogma as temperate analysis.

Installment credit was not a postwar phenomenon. It had played a part, for many years, in the sale of jewelry, furniture, books, pianos, and sewing machines, but these were minor industries and only a moderate percentage of their total sales was made on time. During the twenties, the strategic importance of consumer credit in the automobile industry created the widespread belief that it formed the foundation of the prosperity, a belief that was reinforced by the role that it played in sale of radios, washing machines, vacuum cleaners, and mechanical refrigerators.

Between 1922 and 1929, installment paper outstanding at the end of the year increased from 1,300 to 2,200 million dollars; mercantile open accounts advanced from 1,900 to 2,200 million; total debts arising from personal loans mounted from 2,300 to 4,300 million. In sum, short-term consumer indebtedness increased during the New Era from 6,000 to 9,500 million dollars.

THE ILLUSION OF ECONOMIC STABILITY

In contrast to this rise of 3,500 million dollars in the total indebtedness of consumers, bank deposits increased 16,000 million during this period, a fact that should cast doubt upon the unique importance of installment selling. It can, at best, be contended that the expansion of the consumer durable-goods industries (automobiles and household goods) from an annual volume of 5,600 million dollars in 1922 to 9,100 million dollars in 1929 was greatly affected by the prevalent use of deferred payments. Since new and rapidly growing industries stimulate the economy both directly and indirectly, the above figures probably underestimate the contribution of installment selling to the prosperity of the twenties. But no sophisticated analysis can deal with only one variable. Moralists may insist that the New Era was nourished by the forbidden fruit of consumer extravagance, and that its collapse was retribution for following the evil ways of consuming today and paying tomorrow. Analysts must conclude, however, that installment selling was not responsible for the New Era, though it doubtless sustained and quickened the prevailing prosperity.

APPENDIX II

FOREIGN FINANCING AND TRADE

The United States is conspicuously free from dependence upon foreign trade. It has, therefore, been possible to sketch the outlines of our postwar economy without reference to international factors. Though omission is essential for interpretation, omission always leads to skewness. Although domestic factors may have predominated, the international movement of goods and capital cannot be completely neglected.

Between 1920 and 1929, approximately 1,600 issues of foreign securities were floated in the United States; their net value exceeded 8,500 million dollars. With the single exception of 1923, more than 500 million dollars were raised annually, and during the years 1925 to 1928 inclusive, the billion-dollar mark was exceeded. Of great magnitude, these figures when placed in perspective loom even larger. At the outbreak of the World War, only twelve foreign issues were listed on the New York Stock Exchange and their total annual turnover was less than 4 million dollars. This paltry sum can be explained by the fact that the United States was a capital-importing country; between 1896 and 1914, we borrowed abroad about two billion dollars, while we invested abroad not more than one billion.

Among the major changes wrought by the World War was the transformation of the United States, first, into a capital-exporting country and, latterly, into the world's banker. Between 1915 and 1919, our exports rose from 2 to 8 billion dollars annually, and though our imports likewise mounted, they failed to keep pace. At the beginning of the twenties, the United States had become a creditor nation, but its purchases of foreign bonds during the following years did not represent a mere re-

251

lending of its wartime gains. The cancellation of foreign holdings within the United States had left only a small balance. Like the financing of domestic real estate and securities during the New Era, the purchases of foreign bonds were made with real savings and new money.

The banking system contributed greatly to facilitating the flotation and distribution of foreign securities. Liberal loans to affiliates and to investment houses; the use of correspondent banks as salesmen; direct short-term loans, that were frequently long-term loans in disguise, illustrate the scope of this contribution.

By tradition, by temperament, and by teaching, skeptical of foreign lands, Americans were potentially poor customers for foreign securities. That Iowan schoolteachers, Texan ranchers, and Montana farmers bought bonds of countries whose names they could not even pronounce can be explained only by the expert salesmanship of American financiers.

During the twenties, several of the most important issuing houses were affiliates of commercial banks, a factor that greatly facilitated their securing credit. For instance, the affiliates of the Chase National Bank and National City Bank participated in the sale of no less than three billion dollars of foreign securities. More important was the use of correspondent banks as salesmen. Bonds were allocated to the smaller banks and strong sanctions ensured that they would be purchased. A bank that refused to participate in a particular issue ran the risk of exclusion from all future issues, scarcely a pleasant prospect when one recalls that between 1924 and 1928 ninety per cent of all issues proved profitable. In short, the smaller banks were turned into broker-age houses. Confronted with the task of reselling bonds that they had bought freely or under compulsion, the banks frequently enticed customers by the creation of liberal loans. Not a few foreign bonds remained, however, in their own portfolio; these soon came to be viewed as secondary reserves.

Short-termed loans to foreigners were occasionally made with the understanding that they would be automatically renewed upon expiration. Although Germany reduced her total short-term debt by one-third during 1930-31, American banks still held in October, 1931, more than 650 million dollars of short-term German notes. In part, these loans mere made against goods in transport, but in part they were finance bills with a fictitious maturity. The turn for the worse in world economic conditions in 1929 made the flotation of new foreign securities almost impossible. Hence, loans that had been made to Cuba by the Chase National Bank and the Chase Securities Company could not, as originally planned, be converted into bonds. True, the metamorphosis of short-term into long-term paper occurred, but the bonds were not sold!

Despite the excellent organization of the American banking system for the sale of securities on a large scale—the Liberty Bond campaigns had left their impress—the startling expansion of foreign financing in America during the nineteen twenties must largely be explained in terms of interest rates. Throughout the New Era, foreign bonds had a higher yield than domestic bonds of approximately similar risk. In 1922, the ratio stood at 5 per cent for domestic and 7.5 per cent for foreign bonds; at the end of the New Era, the corresponding figures were 4.5 and 6 per cent. The fact that foreigners did not object to paying a fairly high price for their money, and the further fact that many Americans retained scruples about investing in common stocks, ensured a broad market for foreign bonds. Even Dwight Morrow was surprised to learn, in 1926, that the *Chicago Tribune* listed 128 foreign issues; at the beginning of the decade, only 6 had been listed.

During the New Era, the flotation and distribution of foreign bonds became a mass-production industry. Syndicates were frequently composed of several hundred members; occasionally a single issue was divided among a thousand participants. Nevertheless, control was highly concentrated. Five houses managed or comanaged issues in excess of one billion dollars: J. P. Morgan,

1,800 million dollars; Brown Brothers, 1,700 million; National
City Company, 1,600 million; Dillon, Reed, 1,500 million; Chase
Securities, 1,300 million. Kuhn Loeb, Guaranty Trust, and Lee
Higginson each floated in excess of half a billion dollars, and
Hallgarten, Speyer, and Seligman each managed between 325
and 225 million dollars. Because of comanagership, these figures
contain duplications, but there can be no doubt that these eleven
concerns, especially the first five, were responsible for floating
most of the new issues that were placed on sale between 1920
and 1929. Incomplete data as to sales confirm their strategic
importance: Lee Higginson, 6,500 million dollars; Guaranty
Trust, 5,000 million; Chase, 3,800 million; National City, 3,300
million; Brown Brothers, 2,000 million; Seligman, 1,300 million.

To appreciate the rapid expansion of foreign financing during
the twenties, emphasis must be placed upon competition among
investment bankers. In their testimony before a committee of the
United States Senate in 1931, Thomas Lamont, Charles Mitchell,
and Otto Kahn reiterated that investment bankers were merchants; Kahn went so far as to state that there was no difference
between a banana peddler and a bond salesman, except that
the latter was under obligation to exercise a higher degree of
integrity and judgment. At the same hearings, a governmental
expert testified that the twenties saw the keenest competition
between investment bankers; only J. P. Morgan and Kuhn Loeb
exercised restraint. Evidence was presented that no fewer than
twenty-nine representatives of American financial houses angled
for the privilege of floating a Colombian loan. Business methods
reflected the intensity of competition: relatives of important
politicians were granted large commissions; others were given
lucrative employment; large sums of money were passed to
mysterious strangers.

The quality of the bonds left much to be desired, a fact not
unknown to the well-informed. In 1927, James Brown, senior
partner of Brown Brothers, had occasion to remark to an American official in South America that bankers back home should

avoid the wide-scale distribution of foreign bonds, for these issues were too risky, both as regards interest and principal. His own concern, however, participated in the distribution of two billion dollars of foreign securities!

Since the future is unknown, every investment is a speculation. Mistakes are inevitable. Although many mistakes can be ascribed to fate, others can more easily be blamed on ignorance and cupidity. During the twenties, foreign bonds were offered to the American public by banking houses whose reputations were much better than their character. Few hesitated to publish prospecti with vital data either completely omitted or condensed to the point of unintelligibility. Phrases took the place of facts, and many phrases were misleading to the point of lies. Astute lawyers, with highly sensitized faculties, were alone in their knowledge of the contents.

Because the majority of foreign bonds were either direct or fully guaranteed governmental obligations, American bankers made only half-hearted efforts to control the specific allocation of the moneys secured from the sale of bonds. When an American syndicate made a special effort to control the expenditures of a suspect borrower—Peru—it was frustrated by the claim that such interference would usurp the "sovereignty of a nation." In testifying about loans to countries in Central Europe, James Speyer explained that, although much effort was devoted to determining the utilization of newly borrowed money, such investigations were really irrelevant—for "we cannot control their budget." Occasionally, the borrower was forced to sign contracts for specific purchases, but since the vast majority of borrowers were governments, the technique was limited. As Mr. Strauss of Seligman and Company testified: "But it is almost impossible when dealing with governments to follow up the actual expenditure of the money."

Responsible governments need not have been supervised; but with few exceptions, the governments of Latin America were irresponsible. Although Brazil secured funds for the electrification of a railroad, at the end of eight years construction had not begun. In 1928, Dillon Reed floated a Bolivian loan, the proceeds of which were used as follows: approximately 7 million dollars for the redemption of the floating debt of the government; 5 million on account to Vickers; 4 million for cancellation of deficits and payment of delayed salaries; one million to redeem railroad bonds of a road whose fiscal status was questionable; one million to redeem sanitary bonds; 375 thousand for the building of an electric railroad. Only 2 million were salvaged for new public works, of which more than half was retained by the Minister of War for military activities in El Chaco. Testimony was also offered to the effect that of a 60 million dollar loan to Colombia "only 18 million was properly invested, the balance being filtered out."

When money was spent for the production of new assets rather than for the liquidation of old debts, the spending was frequently lavish. A careful observer estimated that public works in Peru cost double what they were worth, and many were totally unproductive. In Cuba, roads that could have been built for a few thousand dollars were entered on the books at more than one hundred thousand dollars. The bankers did not fail to honor these requisitions, for such action would have "usurped the functions of the Cuban Government." The specific allocation of revenues for the servicing of interest and principal was likewise questionable. In Brazil, the gross revenues of a railroad were pledged, though "the railroad had never operated in its history without a deficit. . . ." Promises were broken with impunity; Peru pledged the revenue from the tobacco monopoly but, as soon as conditions became strained, "the revenues were applied in contravention of the loan."

In sum, foreign financing during the twenties, especially the financing of Latin America, is a tale of avid bankers exploiting ignorant investors. With promises and poverty as collateral, defaults were inevitable. But the rampant optimism of the public, and the criminal recklessness of the banking community, obscured the unpleasant facts and substituted a pleasant illusion.

APPENDIX II

While it lasted, the orgy was pleasant. The flotation and distribution of more than eight billion dollars of foreign securities within a single decade could not fail to enrich investment bankers. More important, it stimulated the economy at large. As Otto Kahn testified, and Thomas Lamont and Charles Mitchell confirmed, it was customary for borrowers to make purchases in the country where they secured their loans. Kahn pointed out that in France this was the rule, and in other countries the custom.

Foreign lending was, therefore, an important determinant of foreign trade. Prior to the outbreak of the World War, our exports averaged approximately 2,500 million dollars annually; by 1919, they were in excess of 8,000 million. During the New Era, the figures varied from slightly under 4 to slightly more than 5 billion dollars annually—in short, a startling increase over our prewar total.

Following the trend established prior to the World War, the composition of American exports during the New Era was heavily weighted with crude materials, semimanufactures, and finished manufactures. Crude and manufactured foodstuffs were relatively unimportant. In 1929, finished manufactures accounted, by value, for half of our exports.

Despite the marked increases in domestic production during the twenties, the ratio of exports to total production increased for the following important commodities: automobiles from 4 to 10 per cent; agricultural machinery from 14 to 22 per cent; cash registers from 8 to 17 per cent; locomotives from 7 to 21 per cent. At the end of the decade, we were exporting 50 per cent of our total production of motor cycles, 40 per cent of our typewriters, and 25 per cent of our sewing and paper machines.

Our industrial prosperity during the New Era was clearly enhanced by our export trade. But the contributions of foreign financing to the prosperity of the twenties cannot by gauged solely by increases in exports. Upon occasion, the stimulation was indirect. Petroleum, telephone and telegraph, radio, electrical, public-utility, and mining companies secured important concessions in Latin America. Although it has been maintained that these concessions were obtained by competitive bidding, only the naïve believe that the banking community was without influence.

The interaction of production, expectations, and money that loomed so large in our domestic economy can also be discerned in our foreign enterprise. Once investors became sanguine about the future of world economic conditions, their coffers opened and the wheels of American industry turned more rapidly. That their judgment was faulty mattered little, for their actions helped to justify their judgment. Impoverished countries serviced old bonds with moneys obtained from new loans. As long as the danger signs were obscured there was nothing to fear. The illusory can defeat the real, but not for long.

NOTES

NOTES

CHAPTER I

[1] Cf. Wesley Clair Mitchell, *A History of the Greenbacks*, Chicago, 1903, *passim*.

[2] Cf. Arthur F. Burns, *Production Trends in the United States Since 1870*, New York, 1934, Appendix A.

[3] *Ibid.* Cf. also David A. Wells, *Recent Economic Changes*, New York, 1898, pp. 18, 82.

[4] *The Stabilization of Business*, ed. by Lionel D. Edie, New York, 1923, p. 330; *Final Report of the Industrial Commission*, Vol. XIX, Washington, 1902, p. 1; *Statistical Abstract of the United States, 1937*, Washington, 1938, p. 372.

[5] Cf. Milton Handler, *Trade Regulation*, Chicago, 1937, Chaps. III-V.

[6] Wells, *op. cit.*, pp. 465-66.

[7] *Fin. Rep. of Ind. Com.*, pp. 31, 485.

[8] *Stat. Abst., 1937*, p. 95.

[9] Cf. Wesley C. Mitchell, *Business Cycles*, New York, 1927, p. 411; Frederick C. Mills, *Economic Tendencies*, New York, 1932, p. 2.

[10] Mills, *op. cit.*, pp. 2, 39ff., 139ff.

[11] Cf. John Maurice Clark, *Strategic Factors in Business Cycles*, New York, 1934, p. 130; Report of Committee on *Recent Economic Changes* of the President's Conference on Unemployment, New York, 1929, p. 464.

[12] Mills, *op. cit.*, p. 188; *Recent Economic Changes*, p. 454; Willford Isbell King, *The National Income and Its Purchasing Power*, New York, 1930, p. 278.

[13] Mills, *op. cit.*, pp. 201, 238ff.; King, *op. cit.*, p. 278; *Recent Economic Changes*, pp. 478, 853-ft. 10.

[14] Cf. Paul H. Douglas, *Real Wages in the United States 1890-1926*, Boston, 1930, p. 445; Investigation of National Bureau of Economic Research for Committee of President's Conference on Unemployment, *Business Cycles and Unemployment*, New York, 1923, p. 59; *Recent Economic Changes*, pp. 454, 464.

[15] *Report of the President's Conference on Unemployment*, Washington, 1921, pp. 15, 25ff.

[16] *Ibid.*, pp. 30, 154, 158; Mills, *op. cit.*, pp. 191-92, 210-ft. 2.

[17] *President's Conference on Unemployment*, pp. 31, 154; *The Annalist*,

January 9, 1922; *Bradstreet's*, January 7, 1922; *Dun's Review*, January 7, 1922.

[18] *Business Cycles and Unemployment*, pp. 27, 29; Mills, *op. cit.*, pp. 194ff., 277-78.

[19] *Facts and Figures of the Automobile Industry, 1921* and *1922*, Nat. Aut. Cham. Com., New York, 1922, 1923.

[20] *President's Conference on Unemployment*, pp. 111ff.; Mills, *op. cit.*, p. 191.

CHAPTER II

[1] *Proc. Aca. Pol. Science*, Vol. IX, No. 4, p. 97.

[2] *Final Report of Industrial Commission* made frequent reference to the costs of seasonality; cf. also *Unemployment in the United States*, Hearings before Com. on Educ. and Labor, Seventieth Congress, Washington, 1929 (hereafter quoted as *S. Res. 219*), pp. 21, 23, where Sam A. Lewisohn estimated the annual loss from seasonal unemployment at 2 billion dollars; *Less Unemployment*, Governor's Commission on Unemployment Problems for State of N. Y., 2nd printing, June, 1931, p. 6: "Seasonal unemployment seems to be the principal single cause of the total volume [of unemployment] . . ."; *Waste in Industry*, Committee on Elimination of Waste in Industry of the Fed. Amer. Engin. Socs., New York, 1921, p. 16.

[3] Cf. *S. Res. 219*, p. 20: "direct, definite, immediate attack . . ."; *Fin. Rep., Special Committee on Stabilization of Employment*, Mass., 1932, p. 101; *Fin. Rep. of Ind. Com.*, pp. 749ff.

[4] *Waste in Industry*, p. 14; *Less Unemployment*, p. 11; Field investigations of writer (hereafter designated #): # Dennison Manufacturing Company, # Hickey-Freeman, # Procter and Gamble.

[5] Reconstructing America, ed. by Edwin Wildman, Boston, 1919, *passim*.

[6] "Unemployment is a problem which Society must solve, and we believe it is better solved by business men than by passing it over to the government for solution." *Less Unemployment*, p. 67; *Recent Economic Changes*, p. 491; *Stat. Abst. 1937*, p. 95.

[7] *S. Res. 219*, p. vi.

[8] Cf., especially, Edwin S. Smith, *Reducing Seasonal Unemployment*, New York, 1931, *passim*. This book is the most exhaustive treatment of the subject; the author has collected data relating to the experiments of more than two hundred concerns.

[9] *Ibid.; Less Unemployment*, pp. 32, 51; # Mazda Lamp Division of General Electric ships approximately 6 per cent of its annual production in July and 11 per cent in November.

[10] *Less Unemployment*, pp. 40ff. # Columbia Conserve; # Hilles Brothers; # Dennison Manufacturing Company.

NOTES

Less Unemployment, pp. 46ff.; Smith, *op. cit.*, pp. 125ff.

[12] Leverett S. Lyon, *Hand-to-Mouth Buying*, Washington, 1929, *passim; Recent Economic Changes*, p. 303.

[13] # General Electric; # General Motors.

[14] # Sears Roebuck; # Eastman Kodak.

[15] *S. Res. 219*, p. 499.

[16] *Less Unemployment*, pp. 13, 79, 80, 86.

[17] *S. Res. 219*, pp. 20, 82; Lewisohn *et al., Can Business Prevent Unemployment?* New York, 1925, p. 3.

[18] *S. Res. 219*, p. 498; Lewisohn, *et al., op. cit.*, p. 57.

[19] *S. Res. 219*, pp. 127-28; *Less Unemployment*, pp. 33-34, 46-47.

CHAPTER III

[1] Cf. F. W. Taussig, *The Tariff History of the United States*, New York, 1931, pp. 65, 366.

[2] Mills, *op. cit.*, pp. 161ff.

[3] Cf. J. Schoenhof, *The Economy of High Wages*, New York, 1892, *passim.* Cf. also, Dostoyevsky, *The Brothers Karamazov*, Modern Library Edition, pp. 960-61—Mitya in discussing the possibility of escaping to the United States remarks: "And though they may be wonderful at machinery, every one of them, damn them, they are not of my soul."

[4] Mills, *Economic Tendencies*, pp. 135, 159; data based largely on Douglas. Cf. also Thomas Nixon Carver, *The Present Economic Revolution in the United States*, Boston, 1925, p. 56.

[5] Douglas, *Real Wages in U. S. 1890-1926*, p. 392.

[6] *Ibid.*, pp. 246, 254, 277ff., 340, 371, 376ff.; Alvin Hansen, "The Buying Power of Labor during the War," Jour. Amer. Statis. Soc., Vol. XVIII, pp. 56ff.

[7] *Stat. Abst. 1937*, p. 300; *Business Cycles and Unemployment*, p. 86; Douglas, *op. cit.*, p. 468.

[8] *Wages in the United States 1914-1929*, National Industrial Conference Board, New York, 1930, pp. 36, 104; *Recent Economic Changes*, p. 432.

[9] Mills, *op. cit.*, pp. 412ff.; Douglas, *op. cit.*, p. 98; *Recent Economic Changes*, p. 435; Professor Wolman points out "union rates . . . fall lower in periods of depression, than the recorded rates indicate."

[10] Douglas, *op. cit.*, p. 392.

[11] *Wages in U. S. 1914-1929*, p. 36; *Recent Economic Changes*, pp. 454-55; Mills, *op. cit.*, pp. 192ff.

[12] *Wages in U. S. 1914-1929*, p. 39; *Recent Economic Changes*, p. 445-ft. 20.

[13] *Recent Economic Changes*, p. 480; Douglas, *op. cit.*, p. 563; cf. W. Jett Lauck, *The New Industrial Revolution and Wages*, 1929, p. 72;

excerpt from speech of Sam Lewisohn: ". . . it is of prime importance that labor does not become resentful and suspicious."

[14] *President's Conference on Unemployment*, p. 154.

[15] Lauck, *op. cit.*, pp. 78ff.

[16] *Amerikareise Deutscher Gewerkschaftsfuehrer*, Berlin, 1926, pp. 181ff., 251ff.

[17] Bertram Austin and W. Francis Lloyd, *The Secret of High Wages*, London, 1926, *passim*.

[18] Mills, *op. cit.*, pp. 243, 246, 270, 272, 278; Douglas, *op. cit.*, p. 445; Ralph C. Epstein, *Industrial Profits in the United States*, New York, 1934, p. 613.

[19] *Recent Economic Changes*, Chap. I.

[20] King, *Nat. Inc. and Pur. Pow.*, Chap. VI.

[21] Lauck, *op. cit.*, Chap. VIII.

[22] *Wages in U. S. 1914-1929*, pp. 39, 41, 43, 48; Douglas, *op. cit.*, pp. 57, 96, 97, 101, 292ff., 550-51; King, *op. cit.*, pp. 146-47; *Stat. Abst. 1937*, p. 316; *Recent Economic Changes*, pp. 436-37.

[23] Simon Kuznets, *National Income and Capital Formation, 1919-1935*, New York, 1937, p. 25.

CHAPTER IV

[1] *Stat. Abst. 1937*, p. 301.

[2] Willard Long Thorp and Wesley C. Mitchell, *Business Annals*, New York, 1926, pp. 127ff.

[3] David Friday, *Profits, Wages, and Prices*, New York, 1921, *passim*; Mills, *Economic Tendencies*, Chap. V.

[4] Mills, *op. cit.*, p. 316.

[5] *Recent Economic Changes*, Chap. IX.

[6] *Ibid.*

[7] *Ibid.*, p. 648; Mills, *op. cit.*, p. 348.

[8] *Recent Economic Changes*, Chap. IX.

[9] *Open-Price Trade Associations*, 70th Cong., 2nd Sess., Sen. Doc. 226, *passim*; Handler, *Trade Regulation, passim;* Arthur Robert Burns, *The Decline of Competition*, New York, 1936, *passim*.

[10] Mills, *op. cit.*, p. 482; Simon Kuznets, *Income Originating in Nine Basic Industries, 1919-1934*, Nat. Bur. Eco. Res., Bul. 59, *passim*.

[11] Cf. the increasing protection afforded trade-marks and trade names; Handler, *op. cit.*, Chap. VI.

[12] Mills, *op. cit.*, pp. 327-28; J. W. F. Rowe, *Markets and Men*, New York, 1936, *passim;* William Yandell Elliott, *et al.*, *International Control in the Non-Ferrous Metals*, New York, 1937, *passim*.

NOTES

[13] Rowe, *op. cit., passim;* Elliott, *et al., op. cit., passim.*

[14] Mills, *op. cit.,* pp. 401, 409.

[15] *Ibid.,* pp. 103, 109.

[16] *Ibid.,* p. 401.

[17] *Ibid.,* pp. 296ff.; Harry Jerome, *Mechanization in Industry,* New York, 1934, pp. 217-18; J. Maurice Clark, *Studies in the Economics of Overhead Costs,* Chicago, 1923, *passim;* Harold G. Moulton, *The Formation of Capital,* Washington, 1935, *passim.*

[18] *Recent Economic Changes,* pp. 862, 874, 910; Epstein, *Industrial Profits,* Chap. III.

[19] *Technical Progress and Agricultural Depression,* Eugen Altschul and Frederick Strauss, Nat. Bur. Eco. Res., Bul. 67, *passim;* Mills, *op. cit.,* p. 348; Kuznets, *Inc. Orig. in Nine Basic Ind., 1919-1934,* p. 22.

[20] Altschul and Strauss, *op. cit.,* p. 4.

[21] *Yearbook of Agriculture 1930,* Washington, 1930, p. 990; W. E. Grimes, "Social and Economic Aspects of Large-Scale Farming in the Wheat Belt," *Jour. Farm Eco.,* Vol. XIII, pp. 21ff.

[22] Altschul and Strauss, *op. cit., passim; Agric. Year. 1930,* p. 988; L. P. Gabbard, "Effect of Large-Scale Production on Cotton Growing in Texas," *Jour. Farm Eco.,* Vol. X, pp. 211ff.

[23] *Recent Economic Changes,* pp. 599ff.

[24] *Ibid.,* pp. 416ff.

[25] Paul Nystrom, *Economics of Retailing,* New York, 1930, Vol. II, p. 121.

[26] Nystrom, *op. cit.,* Vol. I, p. 354; *Operating Expenses of Department Stores* . . . , Bur. Bus. Res., Har. Univ., Bul. 74, *passim.*

[27] *Recent Economic Changes,* p. 362; *Chain Stores: Growth and Development,* 72nd Cong. 1st Sess., *Sen. Doc. 100,* p. xiii; *Chain Stores: Sales, Costs and Profits of Retail Chains,* 73rd. Cong., 1st Sess., *Sen. Doc. 40,* pp. 28-29, 39, 92, 102-103.

[28] *Sen. Doc. 40,* p. 53.

[29] *Ibid.,* p. 52.

[30] Mills, *op. cit.,* p. 482.

[31] *Ibid.,* pp. 401, 484; Epstein, *op. cit.,* p. 68.

[32] Kuznets, *Inc. Orig. in Nine Basic Ind., 1919-1934,* p. 22; Altschul and Strauss, *op. cit.,* p. 2.

[33] Mills, *op. cit.,* pp. 143, 482; Epstein, *op. cit.,* pp. 301, 636.

[34] Mills, *op. cit.,* pp. 490, 496.

[35] King, *Nat. Inc. and Pur. Pow.,* p. 191.

[36] Epstein, *op. cit.,* pp. 149-151.

[37] *Ibid.*, pp. 53, 613; cf. also Chap. XLV where the author discusses the problems involved in the evaluation of assets.

[38] *Ibid.*, pp. 56, 161ff.

[39] *Ibid.,* pp. 114ff., 617ff.

[40] *Ibid.*, pp. 56, 124, 635ff.

[41] *Ibid.*, pp. 42, 68, 172ff.

[42] *Ibid.*, p. 159.

CHAPTER V

[1] *Twenty-Third Annual Report, Federal Reserve Board 1936*, p. 63; Benjamin Haggott Beckhart and James G. Smith, *The New York Money Market*, New York, 1932, Vol. II, Chap. IV.

[2] *Fed. Res. Bd. 1936*, p. 63; Lauchlin Currie, *The Supply and Control of Money in the United States*, Cambridge, 1934, pp. 31ff.; James W. Angell, *The Behavior of Money*, New York, 1936, p. 175. Although the three sources do not agree, the discrepancies are not sufficient to affect the analysis materially.

[3] Edwin Walter Kemmerer, *Money*, New York, 1935, pp. 52-53; James W. Angell, "Money, Prices and Production," *Quart. Jour. Eco.*, Vol. XLVIII, pp. 46, 73ff.; Lauchlin Currie, "A Note on Income Velocities," *Quart. Jour. Eco.*, Vol. XLVIII, pp. 353-54.

[4] *Fed. Res. Bd. 1936*, pp. 124-25.

[5] H. Parker Willis and John M. Chapman, *The Banking Situation*, New York, 1934, pp. 697ff.; Currie, *Supply and Control of Money*, Chap. IV.; Lauchlin Currie, "The Decline of the Commercial Loan," *Quart. Jour. Eco.*, xlv, pp. 698ff.; Mills, *Economic Tendencies*, p. 450; *N. Y. Mon. Mkt.*, Vol. III, pp. 242ff.

[6] *Recent Economic Changes*, p. 682.

[7] Currie, *Decline of Com. Loan, passim.*

[8] *Ibid.*

[9] Willis and Chapman, *op. cit.*, Chap. XXV.

[10] *The Internal Debts of the United States*, ed. by Evans Clark, New York, 1933, p. 71; Charles E. Persons, "Credit Expansion, 1920 to 1929, and Its Lessons," *Quart. Jour. Eco.*, XLV, p. 104; Willis and Chapman, *op. cit.*, p. 590.

[11] Persons, *op. cit.*, p. 106; Willis and Chapman, *op. cit.*, p. 591.

[12] Willis and Chapman, *op. cit.*, p. 556, Chap. XXVI.

[13] *Ibid.*, p. 627; *The Security Markets*, Twentieth Century Fund, New York, 1935, pp. 108ff., Appendix II.

[14] *Ibid.;* John Maynard Keynes, *A Treatise on Money*, Vol. II, p. 197.

[15] Willis and Chapman, *op. cit.*, pp. 568ff.

[16] *The Time Deposit Problem*, B. H. Beckhart, for Com. on Bank. Law

and Practice, Ass. of Res. City Bankers, May 29, 1934, not published, *passim;* Currie, *Supply and Control of Money,* p. 70.

[17] Beckhart, *op. cit., passim; Member Bank Reserves,* Rep. of Com. on Bank Res. of F.R.S., Washington, 1931, pp. 14ff.; Angell, *Behavior of Money,* p. 10.

[18] Bernhard Ostrolenk and Adrian M. Massie, *How Banks Buy Bonds,* New York, 1932, Chaps. II, III, XII; *Fed. Res. Bd. 1927,* pp. 7-8. Cf. below, Appendix II.

[19] Willis and Chapman, *op. cit.,* p. 581.

[20] A. C. Pigou, *Industrial Fluctuations,* London, 1927, Chap. VII.

[21] *Internal Debts,* pp. 76ff.

[22] *Security Markets,* pp. 42, 218, 745, 753.

[23] Simon Kuznets, *Nat. Inc. and Cap. For. 1919-1935,* Table 6.

[24] *Ibid.;* Mills, *op. cit.,* pp. 427, 438.

CHAPTER VI

[1] Nourse and Associates, *America's Capacity to Produce,* Washington, 1934, pp. 41, 120, 228; Mills, *Economic Tendencies,* p. 191; *Bradstreet's, op. cit.,* Vol. L, 1922, pp. 4, 113, 117, 218; *Facts and Figures of the Automobile Industry,* 1921, 1922, 1923 editions, *passim.*

[2] *Facts and Fig. Aut. Ind., 1921-1930, passim.*

[3] *Ibid.,* 1930, *passim.*

[4] *Ibid.,* p. 57; Clark Warburton, "Plateaus of Prosperity and Plains of Depression," *Economic Essays in Honor of Wesley Clair Mitchell,* pp. 503, 508ff.

[5] Mills, *op. cit.,* pp. 191, 264-65; David L. Wickens and Ray R. Foster, *Non-Farm Residential Construction, 1920-1936,* Nat. Bur. Eco. Res., Bul. 65, p. 2.

[6] *Recent Economic Changes,* pp. 224ff.

[7] *Encyclopedia Social Sciences,* Vol. XIII, pp. 56-57.

[8] *Biennial Census of Manufacturing,* 1921; *15th Census U. S., Manufacturing, 1929,* Vol. I; *Recent Economic Changes,* p. 327.

[9] Nourse and Associates, *op. cit.,* pp. 228-29.

[10] John Maurice Clark, *Preface to Social Economics,* New York, 1936, pp. 327ff.; Clark, *Strategic Factors,* pp. 27ff.

[11] Clark, *Strategic Factors,* p. 38.

[12] Thorstein Veblen, *The Theory of Business Enterprise,* New York, 1904; A. C. Pigou, *Economics of Welfare,* London, 1929; John Maynard Keynes, *The General Theory of Employment Interest and Money,* New York, 1936.

[13] Veblen, *Business Enterprise,* p. 187; Pigou, *Industrial Fluctuations,* Chap. VII.

THE ILLUSION OF ECONOMIC STABILITY

[14] A. A. Berle and V. J. Pederson, *Liquid Claims and National Wealth*, New York, 1934, *passim;* Emerson West Axe, "Generally Low Prices and Cheap Money Suggest a Bull Market This Year," *The Annalist*, Jan. 16, 1931, pp. 92ff.; George B. Roberts, "The Price-Earnings Ratio as an Index of Stock Prices," *Proc. Amer. Stat. Ass.*, Mar. 1929, Sup., pp. 22ff.; Herbert F. Boettler, "Post-War Trend of Stock Prices Almost Parallel to Earnings and Dividends," *The Annalist*, Apr. 25, 1930; Robert C. Effinger, "Corporate Earnings and Stock Prices," *Proc. Amer. Stat. Ass.*, 1930, pp. 80ff.; *Security Markets*, Twentieth Century Fund, pp. 176ff.

[15] *N. Y. St. Exchange*, Report of the President, 1926-1927, 1927-1928, 1928-1929, *passim.*

[16] Effinger, *op. cit., passim.*

[17] Veblen, *Business Enterprise*, pp. 201ff.

[18] *Ibid.;* Barbara Wootton, *Plan or No Plan*, New York, 1935, *passim.*

[19] *N. Y. St. Exchange*, Reports of the President for years 1922 to 1929, *passim; Internal Debts*, p. 66; Mills, *op. cit.*, p. 264; *Financial Statistics of Cities*, 1922, p. 266 and 1929, p. 466.

[20] Cf. above, Chap. V.

[21] Willis and Chapman, *op. cit.*, p. 246; Currie, *Supply and Control of Money*, p. 70; D. H. Robertson, *Banking Policy and the Price Level*, London, 1932, Chap. VI; Epstein, *Industrial Profits*, Chap. VI, p. 615.

[22] Moulton, *op. cit., passim;* Clark, *Strategic Factors*, pp. 138-39.

[23] Kuznets, *Nat. Inc. and Cap. For.*, p. 24; Keynes, *General Theory*, pp. 184-85.

[24] Maurice Leven *et al.*, *America's Capacity to Consume*, Washington, 1934, Chap. VI; Clark, *Strategic Factors*, p. 216—"the mere upward movement of per capita income will tend to cause a larger percentage of the increased income to be saved."

[25] *Fed. Res. Bd. 1927, passim.*

[26] Epstein, *op. cit.*, p. 242; Mills, *op. cit.*, p. 482.

[27] Kuznets, *Nat. Inc. and Cap. For.*, p. 24.

[28] *Chase Economic Bulletin*, B. M. Anderson, Vols. II-IX, especially No. 6, Vol. IX.

[29] Leven *et al.*, *op. cit.*, p. 54.

[30] Wickens and Foster, *op. cit., passim; Recent Economic Changes*, pp. 434ff.; Burns, *Decline of Competition*, Chap. V; *Stat. Abst. 1937*, p. 363.

[31] Burns, *Production Trends*, p. 105; Mills, *op. cit.*, p. 264; *Encyclopedia Social Sciences*, Vol. XIII, p. 56.

NOTES

CHAPTER VII

[1] Burns, *Production Trends, passim,* especially Appendix A.

[2] Mills, *Economic Tendencies,* pp. 310-11.

[3] Irving Fisher, *The Stock Market Crash and After,* New York, 1930, pp. 61ff.; *The Chase Economic Bulletin,* Vol. IX, No. 6; *National City Bank of N. Y., Letter,* Jan., 1930.

[4] *Fed. Res. Bd. 1936,* p. 187; Wesley C. Mitchell and Arthur F. Burns, *Production during the American Business Cycle of 1927-1933,* Nat. Bur. Eco. Res., Bul. 61, p. 3.

[5] Field investigations of writer designated #: # General Electric; # Procter and Gamble; # Hilles Brothers; # California Packing.

[6] Cf. above Chap. II; # Columbia Conserve agreed to take back unsold stocks; # Dennison Manufacturing Company established a sizable fund to carry the accounts of Class A dealers; # Endicott Johnson followed a policy grounded in pessimism. Fearful of outstanding accounts, it reduced the time period of payments.

[7] # Dennison; # Hilles; # California Packing.

[8] Several concerns, however, speeded their repair work with an aim to maintain their forces.

[9] *Fed. Res. Bd. 1936,* p. 187; Fisher, *op. cit.,* Chap. II.

[10] *Fed. Res. Bd. 1936, op. cit.,* 184ff.; *Nat. Cit. Bk. N. Y., Letters,* May, July, and September, 1930.

[11] Cf. above Chap. III; quoted by Fisher, *op. cit.,* p. 26.

[12] Leo Wolman, *Wages during the Depression,* Nat. Bur. Eco. Res., No. 46; Leo Wolman, *Wages and Hours under the Codes of Fair Competition,* Nat. Bur. Eco. Res., No. 54.

[13] Wolman, *Wages and Hours C.F.C.,* p. 3.

[14] *Ibid.,* pp. 3-4; Wolman, *Wages during Depression,* p. 3.

[15] Frederick C. Mills, *Prices in Recession and Recovery,* New York, 1936, Chap. III.

[16] # Eastman Kodak; This point of view was developed by an important executive of Remington Rand in a conversation with the late H. Parker Willis.

[17] Mills, *Prices in Recession and Recovery,* pp. 117, 130.

[18] *Ibid.,* p. 128; Moses Abramovitz, "Monopolistic Selling in a Changing Economy," *Quart. Jour. Eco.,* Feb., 1938, pp. 200ff.; # Endicott Johnson; # General Electric; # U. S. Steel; # Procter and Gamble.

[19] Clark, *Overhead Costs,* Chap. XXI.

[20] Solomon Fabricant, *Profits, Losses and Business Assets, 1929-1934,* Nat. Bur. Eco. Res., Bul., 55, p. 1.

[21] *Ibid.,* p. 11; *Fed. Res. Bd. 1936,* p. 182.

THE ILLUSION OF ECONOMIC STABILITY

[22] Fabricant, *op. cit., passim; Stat. Abst. 1937*, p. 291.

[23] Fabricant, *op. cit.*, p. 8; *Commercial and Financial Chronicle*, Vol. 130, Part 1, p. 366.

[24] Fabricant, *op. cit.*, p. 10; Adolf A. Berle and Gardner C. Means, *The Modern Corporation and Private Property*, Chicago, 1932, *passim;* # The president of one of the largest rubber tire companies in the United States tried unsuccessfully for two years to convince his board of directors to take cognizance of changed conditions and revise capitalization accordingly.

[25] Fabricant, *op. cit.*, p. 10.

[26] Henry Hilgard Villard, "The Federal Reserve System's Monetary Policy in 1931 and 1932," *Jour. Pol. Eco.*, Dec. 1937, *passim; Fed. Res. Bd. 1932*, pp. 103ff.

[27] *Fed. Res. Bd. 1936*, p. 125.

[28] *Ibid.*, p. 132.

[29] *Annual Report Comptroller of Currency*, Dec. 2, 1929, p. 109; Jan. 3, 1934, p. 86.

[30] *Fed. Res. Bd. 1936*, p. 132.

[31] Kemmerer, *Money*, p. 53.

[32] Mitchell and Burns, *op. cit., passim;* Wickens and Foster, *Residential Construction, passim; Stat. Abst. 1937*, p. 823; Kuznets, *Nat. Inc. and Cap. For., op. cit.*, p. 24.

[33] Clark, *Overhead Costs*, p. 29.

CHAPTER VIII

[1] *Fed. Res. Bd. 1936*, pp. 184ff.; Franklin D. Roosevelt, *On Our Way*, New York, 1934, Chap. I.

[2] Mitchell and Burns, *Production during Amer. Bus. Cycle 1927-1933*, pp. 3-4; Roosevelt, *op. cit.*, p. xi.

[3] Although Governor Roosevelt advocated during the campaign of 1932 a reduction of governmental costs, he did not give hostage to a completely deflationary policy; his statements about an "adequate money supply" were a clue to a potential expansionary program.

[4] Cf. above, Chaps. IV and VI.

[5] Roosevelt, *op. cit.*, p. 87; Lyon *et al., The National Recovery Administration*, Washington, 1935, Appendix A.

[6] Lyon *et al., op. cit.*, p. 3; *Fed. Res. Bd. 1932*, pp. 16ff.

[7] Kuznets, *Nat. Inc. and Cap. For.*, p. 24; Wage Survey of the California Packing Corporation; Wolman, *Wag. and Hrs. under C.F.C.*, pp. 4-5.

[8] Lyon *et al., op. cit.*, pp. 25, 831; Wolman, *Wag. and Hrs. under C.F.C.*, p. 7; Clark, *Social Economics*, pp. 363-64.

270

NOTES

[9] Fabricant, *Profits, Losses, Business Assets 1929-1934, passim;* Kuznets, *Nat. Inc. and Cap. For.,* p. 24; Lyon *et al., op. cit.,* pp. 761ff.

[10] Lyon *et al., op. cit.,* p. 758.

[11] Frederick C. Mills, *Aspects of Manufacturing Operations during Recovery,* Nat. Bur. Eco. Res., Bul. 56, p. 3.

[12] Frederick C. Mills, *Changes in Prices, Manufacturing Costs and Industrial Productivity, 1929-1934,* Nat. Bur. Eco. Res., Bul. 53, p. 2; Lyon *et al., op. cit.,* pp. 792, 900ff.

[13] Lyon *et al., op. cit.,* pp. 310, 791-92, 847; Mills, *Changes in Pr., Man. Costs, Ind. Prod.,* p. 2; Wolman, *Wag. and Hrs. under C.F.C.,* p. 6.

[14] Witt Bowden, "Employment, Earnings, Production, and Prices, 1932 to January 1936," *Mon. Labor Rev.,* Vol. 42, No. 4, pp. 851ff.; Lyon *et al., op. cit.,* pp. 850ff.; Wolman, *Wag. and Hrs. under C.F.C.,* p. 6.

[15] Mills, *Asp. of Man. Op. dur. Rec., passim;* Lyon *et al., op. cit.,* pp. 797-98.

[16] Lyon *et al., op. cit.,* pp. 812ff.; H. Parker Willis and John M. Chapman, *The Economics of Inflation,* New York, 1935, Part I; Walter S. Landis, *An Engineer Looks at Inflation,* The Duke Endowment, 1933, *passim.*

[17] *Fed. Res. Bd. 1936,* pp. 188-89.

[18] Roosevelt, *op. cit.,* p. 146; Kuznets, *Nat. Inc. and Cap. For.,* p. 14.

[19] Kuznets, *Inc. Orig. Nine Basic Ind. 1919-1934,* p. 24; Roosevelt, *op. cit.,* p. 146.

[20] Clark, *Social Economics,* pp. 229ff.; Lyon *et al., op. cit.,* Appendix A.

[21] Burns, *Decline of Competition, passim;* Lyon *et al., op. cit.,* pp. 563ff., 570ff., 894.

[22] Lyon *et al., op. cit.,* Chaps. XXVIII, XXIX.

[23] Remarks of H. I. Harriman, President of the U. S. Chamber of Commerce, at hearings of the House bill (N.R.A.)—quoted in Lyon *et al., op. cit.,* pp. 23-24.

[24] *Fed. Res. Bd. 1936,* pp. 180ff.

[25] Chicago, Oct. 14th—reprinted in *Democracy Marches On,* Supp. *N. Y. Post,* Nov. 21st, p. 10.

[26] Camden, Oct. 29th—*ibid.,* pp. 14-15.

[27] *Fed. Res. Bd. 1936, op. cit.,* p. 124; Robert Murray Haig, "Facing the Deficit," *The Yale Review,* Vol. XXV, pp. 685ff.; Roosevelt, *op. cit.,* p. 20.

[28] Roosevelt, *op. cit.,* pp. 62-63; D. H. Robertson, "The State and Economic Fluctuation," *Authority and the Individual,* Cambridge, 1937; Lyon *et al., op. cit.,* p. 815-ft.18.

[29] *Fed. Res. Bd. 1936,* pp. 124ff.

[30] Arthur D. Gayer, "Fiscal Policies," *Sup. Amer. Eco. Rev.*, Mar., 1938, pp. 90ff.

[31] Professor J. M. Clark informs me that during the early days of the New Deal lack of confidence in an "automatic revival" was widespread among important consultants of the administration.

[32] *Fed. Res. Bd. 1936*, pp. 184ff.

[33] Alvin Hansen, "The Consequences of Reducing Expenditures, *Proc. Aca. Pol. Science*, Vol. XVI, No. 4, pp. 60ff.

[34] Gayer, *op. cit.*, p. 107.

[35] *Fed. Res. Bul.*, Dec., 1937, pp. 1181, 1245.

[36] *Ibid.*, p. 1245.

[37] *Ibid.*, pp. 1181-82, 1250.

[38] *Ibid.*, May, 1938, p. 396.

[39] *N. Y. Times*, April 15, 1938.

CHAPTER IX

[1] Eli Ginzberg, *The House of Adam Smith*, New York, 1934, *passim*.

[2] *Recent Economic Changes, op. cit.*, pp. ixff.

[3] Albert Abrahamson, article on work relief in *Portland Sunday Telegram, Nov. 14, 1937*; also by same author, "A Former WPA Administrator Looks Back at His Job," *Dun's Review*, June, 1938, pp. 10ff.

[4] Keynes, *General Theory*, Chaps. I, II.

[5] Burns, *Production Trends*, p. 172.

[6] Louis M. Hacker and Benjamin B. Kendrick, *The United States Since 1865*, New York, 1934, pp. 147ff.; *Stat. Abst. 1937*, p. 394.

[7] *Stat. Abst. 1937*, pp. 5, 95.

[8] Wickens and Foster, *Residential Construction, passim*.

[9] *Stat. Abst. 1937*, p. 363.

[10] *Ibid.;* Mills, *Economic Tendencies*, p. 264.

[11] Mills, *Prices in Recession and Recovery*, pp. 378ff.; *Stat. Abst. 1937*, p. 823.

[12] *Stat. Abst. 1937*, p. 364.

[13] Mills, *Prices in Recession and Recovery*, pp. 378ff.; Clark, *Social Economics*, pp. 327ff.; Clark, *Strategic Factors*, p. 192.

[14] Mills, *op. cit.*, p. 191.

[15] Karen Horney, *The Neurotic Personality of Our Times*, New York, 1937, *passim*; Vincent Nolte, *The Memoirs of Vincent Nolte*, New York, 1934, p. 94, relates that in 1806 war between the United States and Great Britain was largely avoided because passions were able to cool during the long period that preceded the convening of Congress.

NOTES

[16] *Fed. Res. Bul., Nov., 1936,* p. 904; Keynes, *General Theory,* Chap. XIII.

[17] Max Weber, "Die protestantische Ethik und der Geist des Kapitalismus," *Ges. Auf. zur Religionssoziologie,* Tuebingen, 1922, *passim.*

[18] *Fed. Res. Bd. 1936,* p. 124.

[19] Clark, *Strategic Factors,* pp. 136ff.

[20] *Fed. Res. Bul., Apr., 1938,* p. 300.

[21] *Ibid.,* pp. 299-300.

[22] James W. Angell, "The 100 Per Cent Reserve Plan," *Quart. Jour. Eco.,* Vol. L, p. 35; cf. also work of Fisher, Niesser, and Simonds.

[23] For purposes of simplification, all considerations of velocity have been omitted, and no effort has been made to differentiate between demand and time deposits.

[24] Clark, *Overhead Costs,* p. 435.

[25] Burns, *Decline of Competition, passim;* Abramovitz, *Monopolistic Selling,* pp. 200ff.

[26] Leo Wolman, *Ebb and Flow in Trade Unionism,* New York, 1936, pp. 85ff., 116ff.

[27] Kuznets, *Nat. Inc. and Cap. For.,* p. 14.

[28] Handler, *Trade Regulation,* Chaps. III-V.

INDEX OF NAMES

Alexander, 244

Bentham, Jeremy, 123

Calvin, 230
Carver, Thomas N., 59

Fisher, Irving, 144
Ford, Henry, 58ff., 153

Glass, Carter, 195
Gompers, Samuel, 25

Harding, Warren, 24
Hoover, Herbert, 5, 24, 33, 43, 58, 151ff., 170ff., 190ff., 225ff.

Keynes, John M., 123

Lubin, Isador, 46
Luther, 230

Marx, Karl, 123, 214, 241

Napoleon, 244
Nye, Gerald, 187

Roosevelt, Franklin, 5ff., 172ff., 182ff., 191ff., 201ff., 212, 262ff., 242

Smith, Adam, 51, 96

Veblen, Thorstein, 103, 123

Walsh, David I., 46
Wells, David A., 17ff.
Wiggin, Albert, 156
Willard, Daniel, 46